The Autumn Garden

The Autumn Garden

A PLAY IN THREE ACTS

by

LILLIAN HELLMAN

Boston

Little, Brown and Company

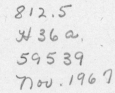

FOR DASH

CHARACTERS

(In order of their speaking)

ROSE GRIGGS	FLORENCE ELDRIDGE
MRS. MARY ELLIS	ETHEL GRIFFIES
GENERAL BENJAMIN GRIGGS	. COLIN KEITH-JOHNSTON
EDWARD CROSSMAN	. KENT SMITH
FREDERICK ELLIS	. JAMES LIPTON
CARRIE ELLIS	. MARGARET BARKER
SOPHIE TUCKERMAN	. JOAN LORRING
LEON	. MAXWELL GLANVILLE
CONSTANCE TUCKERMAN . .	. CAROL GOODNER
NICHOLAS DENERY	. FREDRIC MARCH
NINA DENERY	. JANE WYATT
HILDA	. LOIS HOLMES

The play was presented by Kermit Bloomgarden on the night of March 7, 1951, at the Coronet Theater, New York.

The play was directed by Harold Clurman and the settings were designed by Howard Bay.

The time is September 1949. The place is the Tuckerman house in a summer resort on the Gulf of Mexico, about one hundred miles from New Orleans.

ACT ONE

Monday night after dinner.

ACT TWO

Scene 1: The following Sunday morning.

Scene 2: That night.

ACT THREE

Early the next morning.

The Autumn Garden

ACT ONE

SCENE

THE LIVING ROOM *of the Tuckerman house in a town on the Gulf of Mexico, a hundred miles from New Orleans. A September evening, 1949, after dinner. To the right of the living room is a side porch, separated from the room by a glass door. Upstage left is a door leading into the entrance hall of the house: through this door we can see the hall and staircase. On the porch are chairs and tables. The furniture of the living room is handsome but a little shabby. It is all inherited from another day. (Right and left are the audience's right and left.)*

ON STAGE AT RISE OF CURTAIN

GENERAL GRIGGS, *a good-looking man of fifty-three, is seated at one side of the room reading a newspaper. His wife —*

ROSE GRIGGS, *ex-pretty, soft-looking and about forty-three, is seated at a table wearing an evening dress that is much too young for her. She is chatting across the room with —*

CARRIE ELLIS, *a distinguished-looking woman of about forty-five, who is sitting on a side chair, near her son, Frederick, and her mother-in-law —*

MRS. MARY ELLIS, *in her seventies, sprightly in manner and movement when she wishes to be, broken and senile when she wishes to be broken and senile. She has piled cushions on her chair so she can read a manuscript over the shoulder of her grandson —*

FREDERICK ELLIS, *a pleasant-looking young man of around twenty-five. Occasionally he makes a correction in the manuscript, looks up amused and annoyed at his grandmother. On the right porch —*

EDWARD CROSSMAN, *about forty-six, tired and worn-looking as if he is not in good health, is sitting alone, his back to those in the room. There is a second of silence after the curtain goes up.*

———————

ROSE *(Gets up from her chair. She finds silence uncomfortable and breaks into song "We Stroll the Lane Together").* Now where is it? Everything's been so topsy-turvy all evening. If I can't have it immediately after dinner then I just about don't want it. At home you can bet it's right waiting for us when we leave the dining room, isn't it, Ben? Too bad it's Thursday. I'd

almost rather go and see him than go to the party. *(To*
MRS. ELLIS) I think it's what keeps you awake, Mrs. Ellis.
I mean a little is good for your heart, the doctor told me
always to have a little, but my goodness the amount you
have every night.

MRS. ELLIS *(Pleasantly).* Would you mind telling
me what you're talking about, Mrs. Griggs? You said
if it wasn't for the party you'd go and see *him,* but you
thought *I* drank too much on a Thursday?

ROSE *(Giggles).* Coffee. I mean you drink too
much coffee.

MRS. ELLIS. Then it is coffee you wish to go and
see?

ROSE. Now, now. You're teasing. You know very
well I mean Robert Taylor in that thing.

MRS. ELLIS. Believe me, I did *not* know you meant
Robert Taylor in that thing. You know, General Griggs,
after seven summers I have come to the conclusion that
your wife considers it vulgar to mention anything by
name. There's nothing particularly genteel about pro-
nouns, my dear. Coffee is coffee and not it, Robert
Taylor is Robert Taylor and not him, I suppose, and a
fool is a fool and not her.

ROSE *(Pleasantly).* I know. It's a naughty habit.
Ben has been telling me for years.

(She is close to BEN.)

Do you like my dress, Ben?

GRIGGS. It's nice.

ROSE. Have I too much rouge? *(To others)*
Know what she used to say? *(Quickly)* Ben's mother,

I mean. She used to say it before she died. *(To* CROSS-MAN*)* Come and join us. *(To others)* She used to say that Southern women painted a triangle of rouge on their faces as if they were going out to square the hypotenuse. Ben came from Boston, and his mother was sometimes a little sharp about Southerners.

MRS. ELLIS. Who could have blamed her?

ROSE *(Calling out to* CROSSMAN*)*. Know what she told me last winter when I met her at the Club?

CROSSMAN *(Turns, smiles)*. Ben's mother?

ROSE. No. Your sister, of course. She said we see more of you here on your summer vacation than she sees all year round in New Orleans. She says you're getting to be a regular old hermit. You have to watch that as you get older. You might get to like being alone — and that's dangerous.

MRS. ELLIS. I used to like being alone. When you get old, of course, then you don't any more. But somewhere in the middle years, it's fine to be alone. A room of one's own isn't nearly enough. A house, or, best, an island of one's own. Don't you agree, General Griggs? *(Very quickly)* Happiest year of my life was when my husband died. Every month was springtime and every day I seemed to be tipsy, as if my blood had turned a lovely *vin rosé*.

CARRIE. You're lyrical, Mother.

MRS. ELLIS *(To* FREDERICK*)*. Do you know I almost divorced your grandfather, Frederick? During the racing season in 1901.

FREDERICK *(Looks up, laughs)*. You don't feel it's

a little late to talk about it?

(The phone rings.)

MRS. ELLIS. Thought you might like to write my biography — when you're finished with regional poetry.

(As the phone rings again, SOPHIE *comes into the hall to answer it.)*

SOPHIE *(Into the phone).* No, sir. We do not take transient guests. No, never, sir. Only permanent guests. You might telephone to Mrs. Prescott in the village. Thank you, sir.

ROSE *(Calls into hall).* Dear Sophie, where *is* coffee?

*(*SOPHIE *comes to the hall door. She is a plain-looking, shy girl of about seventeen. She has a hesitant, overpolite manner and speaks with a slight accent. She has on a party dress, covered by a kitchen apron.)*

SOPHIE. Aunt Constance is most sorry for the delay. We bring it immediately.

(She disappears.)

ROSE. Frederick, do you know I've been giving Sophie dancing lessons, or trying to? She's a charming child, your intended, but she's never going to be a dancer.

FREDERICK *(Pleasantly).* Terrible expression, Mrs. Griggs: my intended. Sounds like my indentured. Did you tell Mrs. Griggs, Mother? I thought we agreed that since there were no definite plans as yet —

CARRIE *(A little uncomfortable).* It's natural that I should speak about my son's marriage, isn't it?

ROSE.   Why, goodness, yes indeed it is. I'd have felt hurt —

GRIGGS.   Don't you know that women have no honor, Frederick, when it comes to keeping secrets about marriage or cancer?

FREDERICK *(Looks at his mother)*.   No, sir. I didn't know. I'm too young for my age.

MRS. ELLIS *(Who has been busy reading the manuscript)*.   I know I'm too young to be reading Payson's book. Full of the most confused sex. I can't tell who is what. And all out of doors. Is that new, so much sex out of doors? Is it, General?

GRIGGS.   I don't think it's a question of "new." I think it's a question of climate.

MRS. ELLIS *(Points to book)*.   But aren't sexual relations the way they used to be: between *men and women?* It's so twitched about in Mr. Payson's book. You know, I think the whole country is changing.

GRIGGS *(As if he wished to help* FREDERICK*)*.   Has Payson written a good book, Fred?

FREDERICK.   It's a wonderful book. I think he's going to be the most important young writer —

CARRIE.   You said the first two books were wonderful, Frederick. And they didn't sell very well.

MRS. ELLIS.   I don't know why they didn't — I always thought houses of prostitution had a big lending-library trade.

(FREDERICK *gets up, as if he were angry.*)

CARRIE.   Will this new book sell, Frederick?

FREDERICK.   I don't know, Mother.

CARRIE. I hope it sells. Any man is better off supporting himself.

FREDERICK *(Smiles)*. Mother, sometimes I think no people are quite so moral about money as those who clip coupons for a living.

MRS. ELLIS. And why not? Particularly your mother who is given the coupons already clipped by me who has the hardship of clipping them. That leaves her more time to grow moral. And then, of course, you who don't even have that much trouble are left at leisure to be moral about those who have to go to the trouble of living on unearned money.

CARRIE *(To* GENERAL GRIGGS). You musn't look uncomfortable, General. You should know by this time that my mother-in-law enjoys discussing family matters in public. And the more uncomfortable you look, the longer she will continue.

GRIGGS. Do I look uncomfortable? I was thinking how hard it is to be young.

ROSE *(To* BEN). Won't you come to the party? *(To others)* Ben has never gone to the Carter party. I am sure they're just as insulted every year —

GRIGGS. I don't think so.

ROSE. But what will you do with yourself? Why don't you go to see Robert Taylor? It's that war picture where he does so well and you'll want to see if it's accurate.

GRIGGS. No. I don't want to see if it's accurate.

ROSE. Do you like my dress?

GRIGGS. It's nice.

MRS. ELLIS.   You are a patient man. *(To* ROSE) Do you know you've asked him that five times since rising from dinner?

ROSE.   Well, I feel young and gay, and I'm going to a party. I wish the Denerys would come before we leave. I like meeting new people and they sound so interesting. I thought they were supposed to arrive in time for dinner. *(To* CARRIE) Is he absolutely fascinating?

CARRIE.   I don't know, Mrs. Griggs. I haven't seen him in twenty years or more.

ROSE *(Calling to* CROSSMAN).   Is he fascinating, Mr. Crossman?

CROSSMAN *(Pleasantly).*   You're making it a little harder than usual. Is who fascinating?

ROSE.   Nicholas Denery, of course.

CROSSMAN.   Of course. I don't know.

ROSE.   But, goodness. Didn't you all grow up together? I mean you and Constance and Mrs. Ellis and —

CROSSMAN.   I don't remember any of us as fascinating. Do you, Carrie?

(CARRIE *shakes her head, laughs.)*

(SOPHIE, *carrying a tray with brandy and brandy glasses, comes into the room. She is followed by* LEON, *a young, colored butler, carrying coffee and coffee cups.* FREDERICK *rises and takes the tray from* SOPHIE. *She looks at him and smiles.)*

ROSE.   Let's see your dress, Sophie.

(SOPHIE smiles shyly, begins to take off her apron as LEON pours coffee.)

Oh. It's right nice. But you should wear tighter things, dear.

(Comes in back of her, begins to fool with her hair.)

I'd like to try your hair again.

(SOPHIE moves to help LEON but is cornered by ROSE.)

Now you just sit down. How's this?

(CROSSMAN comes into the room.)

CROSSMAN. Makes her look like everybody else. That's desirable, isn't it?

ROSE. What does Frederick think? We're out to please Frederick, after all, aren't we, dear?

FREDERICK *(Turns to look)*. I like Sophie her own way.

SOPHIE *(Smiles)*. I have no "way."

ROSE. But most European girls have such chic — *(GENERAL GRIGGS gets up, as if he were annoyed.)*

They have, Ben. You said it yourself when you came back from the Pacific, and I was jealous.

MRS. ELLIS. Pacific? I thought you fought in Europe.

GRIGGS. I did. Robert Taylor fought in the Pacific.

(He rises, wanders off to the porch.)

ROSE *(Holding Sophie's hair another way)*. Or is *this* better?

FREDERICK *(Smiles to* SOPHIE*).* Don't you mind being pulled about?

SOPHIE. No. Well. *(Gently pulls away)* I am grateful for the trouble that Mrs. Griggs — Thank you.

CROSSMAN. Sophie doesn't mind anything. All she has said all summer is thank you.

(Through his speech the phone rings. FREDERICK *starts for the phone. At the same time,* CONSTANCE TUCKERMAN *comes through the hall. She is a handsome woman of forty-three or forty-four. She is carrying two flower vases. She puts down one of the vases in order to answer the phone.)*

CONSTANCE. Yes. Just a minute. Frederick. Mr. Payson would like to speak to you.

(She picks up the other vase, comes into the door, as if she were in a hurry. FREDERICK *immediately moves to the phone.)*

Sorry coffee was late. You all want more just ring. And do, Carrie, explain to the Carters why I can't come to their party this year —

ROSE. Any news from them, Constance?

CONSTANCE *(Carefully).* News from whom?

ROSE *(Laughs).* Oh, come now. Stop pretending. When do the Denerys arrive?

CONSTANCE. Don't wait up for them, Rose. You'll see them at breakfast.

(She turns, goes out and goes up the stairs.)

ROSE. My, Constance is nervous. Well, I suppose I should be if I were seeing an old beau for the first time in — But I don't believe in old beaux. Beaux should be brand-new, or just friends, don't you think?

(CROSSMAN *starts out to porch, carrying his coffee and the brandy bottle.* ROSE *points outside, meaning* GENERAL GRIGGS *and* CROSSMAN.)

Now are you boys just going to sit here and share the bottle —

CROSSMAN. General Griggs is only being kind when he says he shares the bottle with me.

(He goes off. FREDERICK comes in, starts to speak, changes his mind.)

CARRIE (Carefully). Was that Mr. Payson on the phone? Is he coming to the party?

FREDERICK. How many generations do you have to summer in this joint before you're invited to the Carters'?

MRS. ELLIS. Oh, that's not true. They're very liberal lately. (Points to ROSE) After all, the last few years they've always included Mrs. Griggs. (To ROSE) And nobody can be more *nouveau riche* than your family, can they? I mean your brother during the war and all that.

ROSE (Giggles). My. Everybody is so jealous of Henry.

MRS. ELLIS. Well, of course we are. I wish we were *nouveau riche* again.

FREDERICK (Sharply). All right, Grandma.

ROSE. Oh, I don't mind. I enjoy your grand-mother.

FREDERICK *(To his mother).*   I'm sorry I'm not go-ing to be able to take you to the party. I hope you'll excuse me, Sophie. Mother. Grandma.

CARRIE *(Carefully).*   What has happened, Freder-ick?

FREDERICK.   Payson had a wire from his publishers. They want the manuscript in the mail tomorrow morn-ing.

(He goes to take the manuscript from the table.)
So I'll have to proofread it with him tonight. It's a nasty job alone, almost impossible —

CARRIE *(Slowly).*   I don't understand.

ROSE *(Hurriedly).*   I must fix my face. As you get older your face needs arranging more often.

(She goes off.)

CARRIE.   We're ready to leave, Frederick.

FREDERICK.   Mother, I'm not going to the party. I wasn't making a joke —

CARRIE.   Oh. I hoped you were. You have no obli-gation to us, or Sophie? An appointment broken, be-cause Payson summons you?

FREDERICK.   I am sorry, Sophie. Maybe I can pick you up later. *(Haltingly)* I *am* sorry.

SOPHIE.   I do not mind, really. It is better this way.

CARRIE.   Don't you? Why not? *(No answer)* Why don't you mind, Sophie?

SOPHIE *(Smiles).*   I do not like parties. I did not

want to go. Now Frederick has some important business and must leave quickly —

CARRIE. Perhaps you are going to make *too* good a wife.

FREDERICK. Suppose you let me decide that, Mother. Good night. Have a good time. See you in the morning —

CARRIE. I want to talk to you, Frederick.

FREDERICK *(Stops, smiles)*. When you use that tone of voice you need two hours. Let's make it in the morning, Mother.

(SOPHIE *has turned away, gone upstage, as if she wanted to be as far away as possible.*)

CARRIE. I ask you to break your appointment with Payson. As a favor to me.

FREDERICK. There's nothing important about my being at the party and it is important to him. He wants to consult me —

CARRIE *(Sharply)*. He is always consulting you. You talk like a public accountant or a landscape gardener. Why should he want to consult *you* about his work?

FREDERICK *(Hurt)*. Maybe because I try to write and maybe because he thinks I know a little. I realize that's hard for you to believe —

CARRIE. I didn't mean that.

FREDERICK. I think you did. Good night.

CARRIE. You have no sense of obligation to me. *(Looks around for* SOPHIE *who is trying at this minute to leave the room)* And none to Sophie. Who evidently won't speak for herself. Do stay here, Sophie, it's your business as well as mine — (SOPHIE *stands still*) I am getting tired of Mr. Payson, Frederick, and with good reason. When he came to stay with us in town last winter, I fully understood that he was a brilliant and gifted man and I was glad for you to have such a friend. But when he followed you down here this summer —

FREDERICK (*Slowly, angrily*). He did not follow me down here and I wouldn't like you to put it that way again. He came here for the summer and is that your business, Mother?

CARRIE. There is just too much of Mr. Payson. Every day or every evening — How often do you take Sophie with you? (*Sharply*) How often have you seen Mr. Payson this summer, Sophie? (*There is no answer*) Please answer me.

FREDERICK. And please stop using that tone to Sophie. Say what you have to say to me.

CARRIE (*Turning to* MRS. ELLIS, *who has been watching them*). Mother —

MRS. ELLIS. I've been dozing. How many hours have passed?

CARRIE (*Slowly*). You are always dozing when there is something unpleasant to face out with Frederick.

MRS. ELLIS. What better time? You all want to know something's been worrying me all day? Nobody in the South has tapeworm any more. In my day that was all you ever heard. Tapeworm, tapeworm, tapeworm. (*Gets up*) Now kiss your mother good night, boy. Otherwise she'll be most unhappy. And say you forgive her.

FREDERICK. I have nothing to forgive her for, Grandma.

MRS. ELLIS. Of course not. But even when your mother starts out being right she talks and talks until she gets around to being wrong.

(She exits. There is silence.)

CARRIE *(Softly).* I'm sorry if I spoke unfairly, or at the wrong time —

FREDERICK *(Comes to her, smiling).* You didn't, you didn't. Now don't feel bad. Nothing's happened. And don't let Grandma tease you.

CARRIE. I know. *(She turns to go)* You go ahead, dear. Try to join us later.

(He kisses her. She smiles, pleased, and goes out. FREDERICK *turns to* SOPHIE.*)*

FREDERICK. Sophie, Mother didn't mean to be sharp with you. But when she is, you mustn't let her. She's a little bossy from time to time, but no harm in it. You look so worried.

SOPHIE *(Very puzzled).* Your mother is not angry now?

FREDERICK. Of course not. You mustn't take these things too seriously. Mother is like that.

SOPHIE *(Smiles).* You know it is most difficult in another language. Everything in English sounds so important. I get a headache from the strain of listening.

FREDERICK *(Laughs).* Don't. It's not worth it. *(Looks at her, then slowly)* Mother is right: I have been rude and neglectful. But I haven't meant to be, Sophie.

SOPHIE.   No, no. You have not been.

FREDERICK.   And in two weeks Mother and I will be going off to Europe. I hope you don't mind about the European trip. It was all arranged long before you and I — *(Stares at her, smiles)* got engaged.

(SOPHIE smiles at him as if she were embarrassed, then she coughs and clears her throat.) We're an awkward pair. I like you, Sophie.

SOPHIE *(Warmly)*.   I like you, Frederick.

FREDERICK.   Sophie, I think we'll have to sit down soon and talk about ourselves. I don't think we even know how we got engaged. We haven't said much of anything —

SOPHIE.   Sometimes it is better not to say things. There is time and things will come as they come.

FREDERICK.   The day we got engaged, we tried to speak as honestly as we both knew how but we didn't say very much —

SOPHIE.   And I think we should not try so hard to talk. Sometimes it is wise to let things grow more roots before one blows them away with many words — *(Shyly touches his hand)* It will come better if we give it time.

FREDERICK.   We will give it time. And you'll make no decisions and set no dates until you are sure about what you think and feel.

SOPHIE.   Oh, I have made the decision for myself. And I am pleased.

FREDERICK *(Pleased)*.   And you are quite sure of your decision?

SOPHIE.   You know, sometimes I have thought that with rich people — *(Very quickly)* with educated people, I mean, decisions are made only in order to speak about changing them. It happens often with Aunt Constance and with your mother, also, I think. And the others.

FREDERICK.   Yes. *(Takes her hand)* We'll get along fine. I want you to know that I feel very lucky —

SOPHIE.   Lucky? You will have to be patient with me. I am not a good success here.

FREDERICK.   Now, you stop that. I don't want you a good success. And you're to stop thinking it. You're to stop a lot of things: letting Mother boss you about, letting Mrs. Griggs tell you what to wear, or pull your hair —

SOPHIE.   Oh, I do not mind. Because I look so bad makes Mrs. Griggs think she looks so good.

FREDERICK *(Smiles)*.   Good night, my dear.

SOPHIE *(Smiles)*.   Good night.

(He exits. SOPHIE *begins to pick up the coffee cups, brandy glasses, etc. After a minute* ROSE GRIGGS *comes down the steps carrying a light summer wrap. She comes in the room.)*

ROSE.   Where are the Ellises?

SOPHIE.   They went to the party, Mrs. Griggs.

ROSE.   No! Without me? I *must* say that's very rude. They can't have done that, Sophie —

(She hurries to the hall, looks out. Then she comes back in, goes to the porch.)

Ben.

(He looks up.)

The Ellises left without me, Ben!

GRIGGS.   Yes?

ROSE.   You'll have to walk me over. I just won't go in, alone.

GRIGGS.   It's across the street, Rose. Not a very dangerous journey.

ROSE *(Gently)*. Ben. *(He rises, comes in)* You know, I think it's shocking. In front of other people. God knows what they know or guess this summer. *(Suddenly notices* SOPHIE *who is collecting cups)* Sophie. Don't wait here listening.

(SOPHIE *turns, surprised, but before she can speak . . .)*

GRIGGS *(Sharply)*.   Rose!

ROSE *(Who is always charming at this point. To* SOPHIE) I am sorry, my dear. Please most earnestly I ask your pardon —

SOPHIE.   Yes, ma'am.

ROSE *(Tries to catch her at door)*.   I'm just a nervous old silly these days. Now say you forgive me —

(SOPHIE *disappears.)*

GRIGGS *(Smiles, as if he has seen this before)*.   All right, Rose. You're charming.

ROSE.   You won't even walk over with me, just to the door?

GRIGGS.   Certainly I will.

ROSE *(Smiles)*. No, you don't have to. I just wanted to see if you would. Will you call for me, at twelve, say?

GRIGGS.   No.

Rose.   Then will you meet me at twelve, at the tavern?

Griggs.   No. What mischief is this, Rose?

Rose.   Is it mischief to want to talk with you?

Griggs.   Again? Tonight? And every night and every day? The same things over and over? We're worn out, Rose, both of us. *(Kindly)* There is no more to say.

Rose *(Softly)*.   No more to say. Do people get divorces, after twenty-five years, by just saying they want them and that's all and walking off?

Griggs.   I suppose some men do. But I haven't walked off and I have said all I know how to say.

Rose.   But you haven't really explained anything to me. You tell me that you want a divorce — And I ask why, why, why. We've been happy together.

Griggs *(Looks at her)*.   You don't believe that.

Rose.   When people get our age, well, the worst is over — and what else can one do? *(Exasperated)* I never really heard of such a thing. I'm just not taking you seriously and I do wish you'd stop talking about it. *(After a pause)* You've never given me a good reason. I ask you ten times a day if there's another woman. I could understand that. Of course you say no, naturally —

Griggs.   There is no other woman.

Rose *(Giggles)*.   You know what I think? I think it's that little blonde at the drugstore, and the minute my back is turned —

Griggs.   Please, Rose. Please stop that.

Rose.   Never at any time, during this divorce talk,

have you mentioned them. You'd think we didn't have sons, and the awful effect on them. Did you write them today?

GRIGGS.   I did not write them because you begged me not to.

ROSE.   Oh, yes, I forgot. It will break their hearts.

GRIGGS.   Their hearts won't be broken. They won't even bother to finish the letter.

ROSE *(Softly, shocked)*.   You can't love them, to speak that way.

GRIGGS.   I don't love them. I did love them but I don't now. They're hard men to love.

ROSE.   Oh, I don't believe a word you say. You've always enjoyed shocking me. You've been a wonderful father and you're just as devoted to them as they are to you.

GRIGGS.   They aren't the least devoted to me — when they think about me it is to find my name useful and when it isn't useful they disapprove of me.

ROSE *(Moving to door)*.   Look, Ben. I just can't stay and talk all night. I'm late now. There's no use our saying the same things over and over again — *(He laughs)* If you won't come to the party what are you going to do?

GRIGGS.   I am going down by the water, sit on a bench and study from a Chinese grammar.

ROSE.   You'll be lonely.

GRIGGS.   Yes, but not for parties.

ROSE.   It's very hard to take seriously a man who spends the evening with a Chinese grammar. I'll never forget that winter with the Hebrew phonograph records. *(Pats his arm)* Now, good night, darling. And don't worry about me: I am going to try to have a good time. We'll talk about all this another day.

(She starts out.)

GRIGGS *(Sharply)*. No. No, we're not going to do that. You're turning it into a pleasure, Rose, something to chatter about on a dull winter night in the years to come. I've told you it isn't going to be that way. *(She is in the hall)* It isn't going to be that way. When you go back to town next week I'm not going with you.

(He turns to see that she has gone.)

ROSE'S VOICE *(From the hall)*. Good night, darling.

GRIGGS *(He stands still for a minute. Then he turns, see his book on the porch table. Goes out to the porch, realizes the doors have been open. To CROSSMAN)*. I guess we thought the doors were closed. I am sorry.

CROSSMAN. Don't be.

GRIGGS. There are so many things I want to do that I don't know which to do first. Have you ever thought about starting a new life?

CROSSMAN *(Smiles)*. I've often thought that if I started all over again, I'd go right back to where I started and start from there. Otherwise, it wouldn't prove anything.

GRIGGS *(Laughs)*. Where'd you start from?

CROSSMAN *(Laughs)*. Nowhere. That's the trouble.

GRIGGS. I started with mathematics. Seems strange

now, but that's why I went to West Point — wonderful mathematics department. So I got myself two wars instead. I want to go somewhere now and study for a few years, or — *(Smiles)* Anyway, sit down by myself and think.

CROSSMAN. Europe?

GRIGGS. I don't think so. Europe seemed like a tourist joint the last time. With all the aimless, dead bitterness of — tourist joints. I don't want sentimental journeys to old battlefields. I'll start tame enough: I've written my sister that I'd like to stay with her for a month or two.

CROSSMAN. Isn't that a sentimental journey?

GRIGGS. I suppose it is. I really want to see her because she looks like my mother. The last six months I've thought a lot about my mother. If I could just go back to her for a day. Crazy at my age —

CROSSMAN. I know. We all do at times. Age has nothing to do with it. It's when we're in trouble.

GRIGGS. I don't know why I want to say this but, well, don't think too badly of my wife.

CROSSMAN. Why should I think badly of anybody?

GRIGGS *(As he turns to go)*. All professional soldiers marry Rose. It's in the Army Manual. She is as she always was. It is my fault, not hers.

CROSSMAN. Haven't you lived in the South long enough to know that nothing is ever anybody's fault?

(GENERAL GRIGGS *laughs, starts out as* CONSTANCE *comes down stairs.* CONSTANCE *has on a different dress and is buttoning the belt as she*

comes into the room. GENERAL GRIGGS *crosses
the room and exits by the stage left windows.*
CONSTANCE *looks around, finds the room is neat,
goes out to the porch, talking as she goes.)*

CONSTANCE. I *think* everything is ready. I've put
Nick in Sophie's room — Sophie says she doesn't mind
sleeping down here. Anyway it happens every summer.
And I've given Mrs. Denery the yellow room. They
wanted *two* rooms, Nick said on the phone.

CROSSMAN. Fashionable people don't sleep together, don't you know that? It's not sanitary.

CONSTANCE *(Sits down).* I'm tired, Ned.

CROSSMAN. Have a brandy.

CONSTANCE. No. It would make me nervous.

CROSSMAN. Remarkable the things that make
people nervous: coffee, brandy, relatives, running
water, too much sun, too little sun. Never anything in
themselves, eh, Constance?

CONSTANCE. They have a maid and a chauffeur.
I'll have to put them in the boathouse. It's all so much
work at the end of the season. Sophie's been cleaning
all day, and I've been cooking — Why did I say they
could come?

CROSSMAN *(Smiles).* I wonder why.

CONSTANCE. Well, of course, I want to see Nick
again. But I am nervous about meeting her. *(Points to
his glass)* Do you think perhaps a sip?

CROSSMAN. Only drunkards borrow other people's
drinks. Have one of your own.

(Through her next speech he pours her a drink

*and hands it to her. When she finishes it, he
will take back the glass and pour himself a
drink.)*

CONSTANCE. I got out Mama's good, old linen
sheets. I don't care how rich the Denerys are, or
where they've been, they never could have had
finer linen. And I've stuffed some crabs and there's
white wine — Remember how Nick loved stuffed
crabs?

CROSSMAN *(Smiles)*. No. I don't remember.

CONSTANCE. It was twenty-three years ago, the
eighteenth of next month. I mean the night he decided
to go to Paris to study. Not so many young men from
New Orleans went to Paris in those days.

CROSSMAN. Just as many young men met rich
young ladies on boats.

CONSTANCE *(Sharply)*. *He fell in love.* People
can't be blamed for changing their hearts — it just happens. They've had a fine marriage, and *that's* given me
happiness all these years.

CROSSMAN. How do you know they've had a "fine"
marriage?

CONSTANCE *(Smiles)*. I know.

CROSSMAN. The rest of us don't know anything
about any marriage — but you know all about one you've
never seen. You're very wise, Constance. It must come
from not thinking.

CONSTANCE. Is this dress all right?

CROSSMAN. You've changed your dress three times
since dinner.

CONSTANCE. My dresses are all so sort of — She'll think they're cheap. *(Smiles.)* Well, and so they are. *(There is silence. Then)* Have we changed much, Ned?

CROSSMAN. Yes, my dear. You've changed, I've changed. But you're still handsome, if that's what you mean.

CONSTANCE. Ned, you don't look so well this summer.

(He is pouring himself another brandy. She points to bottle.)

I wanted to tell you — Don't you think —

CROSSMAN *(Very pleasantly).* Don't I think you should mind your business? Yes, I do.

(SOPHIE comes into living room carrying sheets, a quilt, a pillow, puts them down and moves to porch.)

CONSTANCE. Isn't what happens to you my business?

SOPHIE. You look pretty, Aunt Constance.

CONSTANCE *(To CROSSMAN).* Sophie made this dress for me. Last winter. What could the girls at school have thought? Sophie sitting sewing for an old country aunt when she could have been out dancing —

SOPHIE. I sew better than I dance.

CONSTANCE *(To CROSSMAN).* Sophie's mother taught her to sew. You know that Ann-Marie is a modiste?

SOPHIE *(Laughs).* Oh, she is not. She is what you call here a home-seamstress, or sometimes a factory worker.

CONSTANCE.   But she *designs*. She wrote me and you told me —

SOPHIE *(Laughs)*.   Oh no. You did not understand. She does —

(Outside the house there is the noise of a car coming to a stop. CONSTANCE *turns towards the room, then steps back, moves around the table and suddenly runs into the house.* CROSSMAN *turns to stare at her.)*

SOPHIE *(Timidly, pointing out towards living room)*.   Should I — Should I stay, Mr. Ned?

CROSSMAN.   I don't know the etiquette of such meetings.

SOPHIE.   Why is Aunt Constance so nervous about the visit of this lady and gentleman?

CROSSMAN.   Because she was once in love with Nicholas Denery, this gentleman.

SOPHIE.   Oh. Such a long, long time to stay nervous. *(Sententious)* Great love in tender natures. And things of such kind. *(As he turns to stare at her)* It always happens that way with ladies. For them it is once and not again: it is their good breeding that makes it so.

CROSSMAN.   What is the matter with you?

SOPHIE *(Laughs)*.   I try very hard to sound nice. I try too hard, perhaps?

(She begins to move out into the room; then, as she hears voices, she runs out of the room, exits off porch.)

NICK's VOICE *(Offstage)*.   Constance!

*(*NICK *appears in the hall and comes into the*

room. He is about forty-five, handsome, a little soft-looking and in a few years will be too heavy. He is followed by NINA DENERY, *who is a woman of about forty, good-looking, chic, tired and delicate. She stops and stands in the doorway.)*

NICK *(Calling).* Constance!

*(*NICK *and* NINA *are followed by a maid,* HILDA, *who stands waiting in the hall. She is carrying a jewelry case, an overnight bag, two coats.* CROSSMAN *starts to come forward, changes his mind, draws back.)*

HILDA *(In German).* Shall I take the bags upstairs, madame?

NINA *(In German).* We don't know where upstairs is.

NICK. Oh, I know where upstairs is. I know every foot of this house. *(Examining the room)* It was *the* great summer mansion and as kids we were here more than we were at home — *(Softly)* The great summer mansion! Did the house change, or me? *(Sees* NINA *in doorway)* Come on in.

NINA. Perhaps it would be pleasanter for you to see old friends without me. In any case, I am very tired —

NICK. Oh, now don't get tired. We've just come. What have you got to be tired about? Do you realize how often these days you're tired?

NINA. I realize it very well. And I know it bores you.

NICK.   It *worries* me.

(By this time, NICK, wandering around the room, has reached the porch. CROSSMAN turns and, realizing that he has been seen, now comes forward.)

Could you tell me where we could find Miss Tuckerman?

CROSSMAN.   Hello, Nick. Good to see you.

NICK *(After a second).* My God, Willy. How many years, how many years?

(He puts his arm around CROSSMAN, embraces him.)

Nina, this may be my oldest and best friend in the world. Nina, tell Willy how often I've talked about him and what I said.

CROSSMAN *(Who is shaking hands with NINA, amused).* Then I hope he told you that my name is Edward, not Willy.

NINA *(Amused).*   I hope so — but I am not sure.

NICK.   Your mother always called you Willy. Don't you remember?

CROSSMAN *(Goes out into the hall).*   No. I thought it was my brother's name. *(Calls out, loudly)* Constance, Nick is here.

NICK *(Coming to CROSSMAN).* Tell me before I see her. What has happened here? I don't know anything.

CROSSMAN.   There's very little to know. Old man Tuckerman surprised everybody by dying broke. Constance sold the New Orleans house and managed to hang on to this by turning it into what is called a summer guest house. That's about all, Nick.

NICK. Where is Mrs. Tuckerman? I was crazy about her, Nina: she had style.

CROSSMAN. I don't know where she is, although I've asked myself often enough. She died shortly after Mr. Tuckerman — just to show him anybody could do it.

NICK (*Laughs, pats* CROSSMAN). Good to see you, boy. You know, if anybody had asked me, I would have said this room was as large as an eighteenth-century ballroom and as elegant. I think it shrank. All the fine things were sold?

CROSSMAN. The size hasn't changed. And nothing was sold.

NICK. Could I have been so wrong all these years? Seems so shabby now and —

NINA (*Quickly*). I think it is a pleasant room.

NICK. Does Sam live here?

CROSSMAN. Sam died during the war. He went to Europe, oh, in the thirties, married there and never came back. You'll meet his daughter. Constance imported her five years ago.

NICK. Well, Sam was always the devoted brother until it came to being devoted. And Constance sacrificed her life for him.

CROSSMAN (*To* NINA). Nick is still a Southerner. With us every well-born lady sacrifices her life for something: a man, a house, sometimes a gardenia bush. Is it the same where you come from?

NINA (*Smiles*). New York is too cold for gardenias.

(Through CROSSMAN'S *speech,* CONSTANCE *appears in the hall. As she moves into the room, she trips, recovers herself, smiles nervously and waits for* NICK *to come to her. He takes her face in his hands and kisses her. Then he stands back to look at her.)*

NICK.   This is a good hour of my life, Constance.

CONSTANCE *(Softly).*   And of mine.

NICK *(Holds her face).*   You've changed and you've changed well. Do you still have the portrait, Constance?

CONSTANCE *(Smiles). Still* have the portrait! It's the only important thing I have got —

(Then she remembers NINA, *becomes confused, moves away from him and comes to* NINA.)

Forgive me, Mrs. Denery.

NINA *(Puts out her hand, warmly).*   Hello.

CONSTANCE *(Flossy).*   I should have been here to make you as welcome as you truly are. I was reading when you arrived, reading a book, and I didn't hear the car.

(She sees CROSSMAN *is staring at her and she looks nervously away from him.)*

NICK.   I had expected you standing in the driveway with the sun in your face, in the kind of lovely pink thing you used to wear —

NINA.   The sun is not usually out at night — even for you.

NICK *(To* CONSTANCE*).*   Instead, you are reading. As if you were waiting for the groceries to come.

CONSTANCE *(Quickly).*   I wasn't reading. It was a

silly lie. I was just pretending — *(Embarrassed)* Well, I'm even forgetting my manners. You must be hungry, Mrs. Denery, and I've got —

NICK *(Laughs, takes her hands, pulls her to the couch)*. No, no. Stop your manners, girl. There's a great deal I want to know.

(They sit down.)

Now. Is the portrait as good as I remember it? I want Nina to see it. Nina knows a great deal about painting. Sometimes I think she knows more than I.

CONSTANCE *(Smiles to NINA, nods. Then to NICK)*. You know, Nick, I subscribe to the New York Sunday *Times*. Because of the art section. I wanted to follow your career.

NICK *(Carefully)*. You haven't often found me in the *Times*. I've only exhibited in Europe.

CONSTANCE *(Relieved)*. Oh. That explains it.

(There is a slight, awkward pause.)

I like painting. I like Renoir best. The summer ladies in the gardens, so very, very pretty.

NICK *(Bored)*. Yes, very pretty. This is the same wonderful place — My God, we had happy summers here, all of us. We loved each other so very much. Remember, Ned?

CROSSMAN. I don't remember that much love.

NINA *(Laughs)*. I like you, Mr. Crossman.

NICK. Of course you like him. These are my oldest friends. I think as one grows older it is more and more necessary to reach out your hand for the sturdy old vines you knew when you were young and let them lead you back to the roots of things that matter.

(NINA *coughs.* CROSSMAN *moves away, smiling.*
Even CONSTANCE *is a little overwhelmed.*)

Isn't that true, Ned? Now what have you been up to all these years?

CROSSMAN.   I still work in the bank and come here for my vacation. That's about all.

NICK.   I bumped into Louis Prescott in Paris a couple of years ago and he told me you and Constance had never married —

(Pats CONSTANCE'S *hand;* CONSTANCE *looks embarrassed.)*

Couldn't understand it. No wonder you drink too much, Ned.

CROSSMAN.   Louis Prescott go all the way to Paris to tell you that?

NICK *(Anxious, gets up).*   Oh, look old boy. I didn't mean anything — I drink too much myself. I only want to know about you and have you know about me. I hope you didn't mind, Ned.

CROSSMAN.   Not a bit. I want to know about you, too. Ever had syphilis, Nick? Kind of thing one has to know right off, if you understand me.

CONSTANCE *(Gets up, very disturbed).*   Ned, how can you speak that way?

NICK *(Smiles).*   You've grown edgy. I didn't remember you that way.

CROSSMAN *(Pleasantly).*   Oh, I don't think I've changed. See you in the morning.

NICK.   Hope you'll take me around, show me all the old places —

CROSSMAN.   Of course I will. Good night, Mrs. Denery.

(He exits up staircase.)

NICK *(To* CONSTANCE, *meaning* CROSSMAN*).* I'm sorry if I said anything —

CONSTANCE.   You know, for years I've been meeting you and Mrs. Denery — in my mind, I mean — and I've played all kinds of roles. Sometimes I was the dignified old friend, and sometimes I was a very, very old lady welcoming you to a gracious table. It was so important to me — our first meeting — *(Sadly)* And now when it happens —

NICK *(Heartily).* Nonsense. My home-coming is just as it should be. It's as if I had gone away yesterday. We took up right where we left off: even Ned and I. Let us be as we were, my dear, with no years between us, and no pretending.

CONSTANCE *(Delighted with him, warmly).* Thank you.

(Goes to NINA.*)*

All these years I wanted to write you. I did write but I never sent the letters. It seemed so intrusive of me. I could see you getting the letter and just not knowing who I was.

NICK.   I told Nina about you the first night I met her and through the years she has done quite a little teasing — You are too modest, Constance. *(Suddenly)* Now are you going to let me do another portrait of you?

CONSTANCE *(Laughs)*. Another portrait? No, no, indeed. I want to remember myself as I was in the picture upstairs.

NICK.   Go and get it for me. I want to look at it with you.

(She smiles, exits. There is silence.)
You haven't been too warm or gracious, Nina.

NINA.   What can I do when I don't even know the plot?

NICK.   What are you talking about?

NINA.   You told me about Constance Tuckerman the first night we met? And about dear Willy or Ned, and I've done quite a little teasing about her all these years?

NICK.   I did tell you about her immediately —

NINA.   You mentioned her very casually, last week, years after the night you met me and you said that you could hardly remember anything more about her than a rather silly —

NICK *(Quickly)*. Are you going to be bad-tempered for our whole visit here? For years I've looked forward to coming back —

(NINA laughs.)

NINA.   So you came to do her portrait?

NICK.   No, I didn't "come to do her portrait." I thought about it driving down here. If the one I did is as good as I remember, it would be wonderful for the show. The young girl, the woman at forty-five. She's aged. Have we changed that much? I don't think you've changed, darling.

NINA.   I've changed a great deal. And I wouldn't want it pointed out to me in a portrait to be hung side by side with a picture of what I used to be. *(He doesn't answer her)* That isn't a nice reason for being here and if I had known it —

NICK.   We have no "reason" for being here. I just wanted to come back. Nothing mysterious about it —

NINA.   You're simply looking for a new area in which to exercise yourself. It has happened many, many times before. But it *always* happens when we return from Europe and spend a month in New York. It's been too important to you, for many years, that you cannot manage to charm my family. And so, when our visit is finished there, you inevitably look around for — Well, you know. You know what's been and the trouble.

NICK *(Cheerfully).*   I don't know what the hell you're talking about.

NINA.   I'm tired of such troubles, Nick —

NICK.   Do you know that these sharp moods of yours grow more sharp with time? Now I would like to have a happy visit here. But if something is disturbing you and you'd prefer not to stay, I'll arrange immediately —

NINA *(As if she were a little frightened).*   I'd only prefer to go to bed. Sorry if I've been churly about your — home-coming.

(She starts out, meets CONSTANCE *who comes in carrying portrait.)*

Will you excuse me, Constance? The long drive gave me a headache.

CONSTANCE. I am sorry. Will I bring you a tray upstairs?

NINA. No, thank you.

(CONSTANCE *moves as if to show her the way.*)

NICK. Come, I want to see the picture. Nina will find her way.

(He takes the picture from CONSTANCE.*)*

CONSTANCE. The yellow room on the left. Your maid is unpacking. I peeked in. What lovely clothes. Can I come and see them tomorrow?

NINA *(Going up the stairs).* Yes, of course. Thank you and good night.

(CONSTANCE *watches her and then comes into room.*)

NICK *(Who is looking at the picture).* I was nervous about seeing it. Damn good work for a boy eighteen.

CONSTANCE. You were twenty-two, Nick.

NICK. No, I wasn't. I —

CONSTANCE. You finished it the morning of your birthday. *(She points to windows)* And when you put down your brushes you said damn good work for a boy of twenty-two, and then you asked me to marry you. Don't you remember — *(She stops, embarrassed)* Why should you remember? And I don't want to talk that way.

NICK *(Who is preoccupied with the picture).* Oh, nonsense. Talk any way you like. We were in love,

very much in love, and why shouldn't we speak of
it?

CONSTANCE *(Hastily, very embarrassed).* After I
die, the picture will go to the Delgado Museum.

NICK *(Laughs).* I want to borrow it first. I'm having a retrospective show this winter, in London. I've
done a lot of fancy people in Europe, you know that,
but I'll be more proud of this — And I want to do another portrait of you as you are now. *(Moves toward
window, excited)* You standing there. As before. Wonderful idea; young girl, woman at — Be a sensation.
Constance, it's fascinating how faces change, mold firm
or loose, have lines that start in youth and —

CONSTANCE *(Amazed).* Oh, Nick. I don't want
to see myself now. I don't want to see all the changes.
And I don't want other people to stand and talk about
them. I don't want people to laugh at me or pity me.
(Hurt) Oh, Nick.

NICK. I see. *(Turns)* Well, it would have meant a
lot to me. But that's that. I'll be off to bed now —

CONSTANCE *(Coming after him).* But we haven't
had a minute. And I have supper all ready for
you —

NICK. Good night, my dear.

CONSTANCE *(Slowly).* You think I'm being selfish
and vain? I mean, am I the only woman who wouldn't
like —

NICK. No, I think most women would feel the
same way.

(He starts out.)

CONSTANCE. Do you prefer breakfast in bed? And what shall I make for your dinner? Pompano —

(He is at the door as CARRIE *and* ROSE *come into the hall.* CARRIE *is holding* ROSE'S *arm.)*

CARRIE. Hello, Nick.

NICK *(Takes her hands).* My God, Carrie. I didn't know you were here. How come? It's wonderful —

CARRIE. We come every summer.

NICK. You're handsome, Carrie. But you always were.

CARRIE *(Smiles).* And you always remembered to say so. (ROSE *coughs delicately)* This is Mrs. Griggs. *(To* CONSTANCE) Mrs. Griggs didn't feel well, so I brought her home. She became a little dizzy, dancing.

ROSE *(To Nick, who is shaking hands with her).* You're a famous gentleman in this town, sir, and I've been looking forward so to seeing you. We lead dull lives here, you know —

NICK *(Laughs).* *You* don't look as if you do.

ROSE. Oh, thank you. But I don't look well tonight. I became suddenly a little ill —

CARRIE *(Tartly).* Yes. Well, come along. If you still feel ill.

NICK. Can I help you, Mrs. Griggs?

ROSE *(Delighted).* Oh, thank you. That would be nice. I haven't been well this summer —

*(*NICK *starts into hall.)*

CONSTANCE. Nick —

(He pays no attention. CARRIE *moves quickly ahead of him, takes* ROSE'S *arm.)*

CARRIE. Come. Good night, Nick. I look forward to seeing you in the morning. Hope you're staying for a while.

NICK. I think we'll have to leave tomorrow.

ROSE. Oh, don't do that. *(Then)* Constance, if Ben comes in would you tell him I was taken ill?

*(*CARRIE *impatiently pushes her ahead and up the steps.)*

NICK *(Meaning* ROSE*).* Pretty woman, or was. *(Looks at* CONSTANCE*)* What is it, Con?

CONSTANCE. How can you talk of leaving tomorrow? *(He doesn't answer)* Don't be mad with me, Nick.

NICK. I don't get mad, darling.

CONSTANCE *(Catches him as he is almost out the door).* Please, Nick, please let me change my mind. You are welcome to take this picture and I am flattered you wish to do another. But I'll have to pose early, before they're all down for breakfast —

NICK *(Turns casually).* Good. We'll start in the morning. Do you make a living out of this place, darling?

CONSTANCE *(Gaily).* Not much of one. The last few years have been a little hard. I brought Sam's daughter from Europe — she and her mother went through the occupation and were very poor — and I've tried to send her to the best school and then she was to make her debut only now she wants to get married, I think, and —

NICK.   The girl expected all that from you?

CONSTANCE.   Oh, no. Her mother didn't want to come and Sophie didn't want to leave her mother. I finally had really to *demand* that Sam's daughter was not to grow up — Well, I just can't describe it. At thirteen she was working in a fish store or whatever you call it over there. I just *made* her come over —

NICK.   Why didn't you ever marry Ned?

CONSTANCE.   I can't answer such questions, Nick. Even for you.

NICK.   Why not? I'd tell you about myself or Nina.

CONSTANCE.   Oh, it's one thing to talk about lives that have been good and full and happy and quite another — Well, I don't know. We just never did marry.

NICK *(Bored)*.   Well, then, tomorrow morning. I'll do a good portrait of you because it's the face of a good woman —

(He stops as SOPHIE *comes in. She sees* NICK *and* CONSTANCE *and draws back a little.)*

CONSTANCE.   Sophie. (SOPHIE *comes into the room)* This is Sam's daughter.

NICK *(Very warmly to Sophie)*.   I've been looking forward to meeting you for many years.

*(*CONSTANCE *turns, puzzled.)*

SOPHIE.   How do you do, sir?

NICK.   You follow in the great tradition of Tuckerman good looks.

SOPHIE.   Er. Er.

CONSTANCE *(Smiles)*.   Don't er, dear.   Say thank
you.   (GRIGGS *enters from left porch*) Do come in.
(GRIGGS *comes in*) This is General Griggs.   My very
old friend, Nicholas Denery.

NICK.   Are you General Benjamin Griggs? I've
read about you in Raymond's book and Powell's.

GRIGGS *(As they shake hands)*.   I hear they disagree
about me.

NICK.   We almost met before this.   When your
boys marched into Paris.   I was in France during the
German occupation.

                    (SOPHIE *turns sharply.*)

GRIGGS.   That must have been unpleasant for
you.

NICK.   Yes, it was.   But in the end, one has to be
just; the Germans were damn smart about the French.
They acted like gentlemen.

GRIGGS *(Pleasantly)*.   That's a side of them I didn't
see.   *(Looks over at* SOPHIE*)* You didn't either,
Sophie?

(During his speech HILDA*, the maid, appears
in the doorway.)*

HILDA *(In German)*.   Excuse me, Mr. Denery. Mrs.
Denery would like you to come for a minute before you
retire.   She has a little surprise gift she bought for you
in New Orleans.

NICK *(In German)*.   No.   Tell Mrs. Denery I will

see her in the morning. Tell her to take a sleeping pill.

HILDA *(In German).*   Thank you, sir.

CONSTANCE *(Who hasn't understood the German but who is puzzled because* SOPHIE *is frowning and* GRIGGS *has turned away).*   Can I — Does Nina want something?

NICK.   No, no. She's fine.

(SOPHIE *begins to make up the couch.* NICK *turns to her.)*

That means one of us must have put you out of your room. I'm sorry and I thank you.

SOPHIE.   Not at all, sir. It is nothing.

NICK *(Comes to her).*   You're a sweet child and I look forward to knowing you. Good night. *(To* GRIGGS*)* Good night, sir. A great pleasure. (GRIGGS *bows.* NICK *kisses* CONSTANCE*)* Wonderful to be here, darling.

(He goes out. CONSTANCE *moves to help* SOPHIE *make up the couch. There is silence for a minute while they arrange the bedclothes.* GRIGGS *watches them.)*

CONSTANCE.   I suppose I shouldn't ask but what did the German maid want? Something from the kitchen or — *(No answer)* Sophie. *(No answer)* Sophie.

SOPHIE *(Slowly).*   Mrs. Denery wanted to say good night to Mr. Denery.

GRIGGS.   Mrs. Denery had bought a little gift for him in New Orleans and wanted to give it to him.

CONSTANCE.   After all these years. To have a little
gift for him. Isn't that nice? *(She looks at* GRIGGS *and*
SOPHIE. *Neither answers her. She becomes conscious of
something strained)* What did Nick say?

SOPHIE.   He said she should take a sleeping pill
and go to sleep.

CONSTANCE.   Just like that?

SOPHIE.   Down at the beach there is the frank-
furter concession. I think I will get the sleeping-pill
concession and grow very rich.

CONSTANCE. Why, Sophie. Are you disturbed
about something, dear? *(Looks at her dress)* You didn't
go to the party! I've been so busy, I didn't realize —
Why, where's Fred and —

SOPHIE.   I did not wish to go to the party, Aunt
Constance. And Frederick had a most important appointment.

CONSTANCE. More important than being with
you? Young people get engaged and act toward each
other with such — I don't know. *(To* GRIGGS*)* In our day
we made marriage more romantic and I must say I
think we had more fun. If you can't have fine dreams
now, then when can you have them? *(Pats* SOPHIE*)*
Never mind. I guess the new way is more sensible. But
I liked our way better. *(To* GRIGGS*)* Didn't you? Oh,
what's the matter with me? I forgot. Rose came back
from the party. She said she was ill. I mean, I think
she just didn't feel well — Carrie is upstairs with her.
(He doesn't move) I think Carrie probably wants to go
back to the party and is waiting for you to come.

GRIGGS.   Yes. Of course. Thank you. Good night.
  (He exits.)

CONSTANCE *(She kisses* SOPHIE). You'll be comfortable? See you in the morning, dear.
  (She exits through the hall. SOPHIE *finishes with the couch, goes out. After a second,* CROSSMAN *comes down the stairs. He sticks his head in the door, sees nobody, crosses the room, goes out to the porch, takes the bottle of brandy and a glass, moves back into the room and crosses it as* SOPHIE *returns carrying pajamas and a robe.)*

CROSSMAN *(His voice and his manner are slightly different now).* I needed another book and another bottle. Royalty gone to bed? Does anybody improve with age? Just tell me that, Sophie, and I'll have something to lie awake and think about.

SOPHIE.   I do not know, Mr. Ned.

CROSSMAN.   For God's sake, Sophie, have an opinion about *something*. Try it, and see what comes out.

SOPHIE *(Laughs).*   Some people improve with age, some do not.

CROSSMAN *(Nods, amused).*   Wonderful, Sophie, wonderful. Some improve with age, some do not. Medical statistics show that 61 per cent of those who improve have bought our book on Dianetics and smoke Iglewitz cigarettes. You're beginning to talk like an advertisement, which is the very highest form of American talk. *(Sharply)* It's not *your* language, nor your native land.

You don't have to care about it. You shouldn't even understand it.

SOPHIE. Sometimes I understand.

CROSSMAN. That's dangerous to admit, Sophie. You've been so busy cultivating a pseudo-stupidity. Not that you'd ever be a brilliant girl, but at least you used to be normal. Another five years and you won't be *pseudo*-stupid.

SOPHIE *(Smiles)*. I will not mind. It will be easier. *(Carefully)* You notice me too much, Mr. Ned. Please do not feel sorry or notice me so much.

CROSSMAN. You came here a nice little girl who had seen a lot of war and trouble. You had spirit, in a quiet way, and you were gay, in a quiet way, which is the only way women should be gay since they are never really gay at all. Only serious people are ever gay and women are very seldom serious people. They are earnest instead. But earnestness has nothing to do with seriousness. · So. *(Suddenly)* What the hell is this marriage business between you and Fred Ellis?

SOPHIE *(Softly)*. It is the marriage business between me and Fred Ellis.

CROSSMAN. But what's the matter with you? Haven't you got sense enough to know —

SOPHIE *(Quickly)*. I do the best I can. I do the best I can. And I thank you for worrying about me, but you are an educated man with ideas in English that I am not qualified to understand.

CROSSMAN. Listen to me, Sophie. Sometimes when I've had enough to drink — just exactly enough — I feel as if I were given to understand that which I may not understand again. And sometimes then — but rarely — I have an urge to speak out. Fewer drinks, more drinks, and I'm less certain that I see the truth, or I get bored, and none of my opinions and none of the people and issues involved seem worth the trouble. Right now, I've had just enough: so listen to me, Sophie. I say turn yourself around, girl, and go home. Beat it quick.

SOPHIE. You take many words to say simple things. All of you. And you make the simple things — like going to sleep — so hard, and the hard things — like staying awake — so easy. Go home, shall I? Just like that, you say it. Aunt Constance has used up all her money on me, wasted it, and for why and what? How can I go home?

CROSSMAN. If that's all it is I'll find you the money to go home.

SOPHIE *(Wearily).* Oh, Mr. Ned. We owe money in our village, my mother and I. In my kind of Europe you can't live where you owe money. Go home. Did I ever want to come? I have no place here and I am lost and homesick. I like my mother, I — Every night I plan to go. But it is five years now and there is no plan and no chance to find one. Therefore I will do the best I can. *(Very sharply)* And I will not cry about it and I will not speak of it again.

CROSSMAN *(Softly, as if he were moved).* The best you can?

SOPHIE. I think so. *(Sweetly)* Maybe you've

never tried to do that, Mr. Ned. Maybe none of you
have tried.

CROSSMAN.   Sophie, lonely people talking to each
other can make each other lonelier. They should be
careful because maybe lonely people are the only people
who can't afford to cry. I'm sorry.

*(He exits through the hall, goes up the stairs
as the curtain falls.)*

CURTAIN

ACT TWO

Scene One

SCENE:

> THE SAME AS ACT ONE. *A week later, eight-thirty Sunday morning.*

AT RISE:

> CONSTANCE *is standing against the outside edge of the porch, leaning on the railing.* NICK *is standing in front of an easel.* CONSTANCE *has on a most unbecoming house dress and her hair is drawn back tight. She looks ten years older. In the living room,* SOPHIE *has finished folding her bedclothes and is hurrying around the room with a carpet sweeper. After a second,* LEON *appears from the direction of the dining room with a tray and dishes and moves out to the porch. He puts down the tray, moves the table, begins to place the dishes.* CONSTANCE *tries desperately to ask him if everything is all right in the kitchen. She does this by moving her lips and trying not to move her head.* LEON *sees her motions but doesn't understand what*

*she is trying to say. The noise of the rattling
dishes, and the carpet sweeper, becomes sharp.*

NICK. Constance, please ask them to stop that
noise. *(Waves his hand to* LEON *and* SOPHIE*)* Go away,
both of you.

CONSTANCE. They can't, Nick. I explain it to you
every morning! We simply have to get ready for breakfast. *(Quietly)* Sophie, is everything all right in the
kitchen?

SOPHIE. Yes, ma'am. Everything is fine.

NICK *(To* CONSTANCE, *sharply)*. Please keep the
pose. Just a few minutes more.

CONSTANCE *(To* LEON*)*. Tell Sadie not to cook the
liver until everybody is downstairs, like she always does.
Did she remember about the grits this Sunday? *(To*
NICK, *sees his face)* All right. I'm sorry. But really, I
can't run a boardinghouse and pose for —

(She sighs, settles back. SOPHIE *picks up her
bedclothes and exits through the hall.* LEON
finishes with the porch table and comes back
into the living room as* MRS. ELLIS *comes down
the steps.)*

MRS. ELLIS *(To* LEON*)*. My breakfast ready?

LEON. No, ma'am. We'll ring the bell.

MRS. ELLIS. What's the matter with my breakfast?

LEON. Nothing the matter with it. It will be like
always.

MRS. ELLIS. It gets later and later every day.

LEON.   No, ma'am. That's just you. Want it in the dining room or on the porch?

MRS. ELLIS.   Too damp on the porch. Whole house is damp. I haven't slept all summer, Leon.

LEON.   Just as well not to sleep in summer.

MRS. ELLIS *(As* LEON *exits)*.   You're going to have to explain that to me sometime. *(She turns, goes toward porch, comes around in front of* CONSTANCE*)* Constance, he's made you look right mean and ten years older. Why have you done that, Nicholas?

> (SOPHIE *comes back into living room with a large urn of coffee and small cups. She puts the tray on a table.)*

NICK *(To* MRS. ELLIS*)*.   Shoo, shoo. This is forbidden ground.

MRS. ELLIS *(Calls)*.   Sophie, give me a cup. I have to stay awake for church. *(To* CONSTANCE*)* Ten years older. When you pay an artist to paint your portrait he makes you ten years younger. I had my portrait done when I was twenty-one, holding my first baby. And the baby looked older than I did. Was rather a scandal or like those people in Tennessee.

NICK.   You know if you wouldn't interrupt me every morning, I think I'd fall in love with you.

MRS. ELLIS *(She goes toward* SOPHIE *to get her coffee. During her speech,* SOPHIE *puts three spoons of sugar in the small cup)*.   I wouldn't like that. Even if I was the right age I wouldn't like it. Although I realize it would make me dangerously different from every other woman in the world. You would never have been my dish of tea, and isn't that a silly way of saying it? *(To* SOPHIE: *she is now in the living room)* You're the only one who ever remembers about my sugar. Sophie, will you come up to town (CROSSMAN *comes down the steps and into the room)* and stay with me for a few weeks while Carrie and Frederick are in Europe?

SOPHIE. I would like that.

MRS. ELLIS. Ned, what shall I give Sophie for her wedding present? My pearls or my mother's diamonds?

CROSSMAN *(To* SOPHIE). The rich always give something old and precious to their new brides. Something that doesn't cost them new money. Same thing true in your country?

SOPHIE *(Smiles).* I do not know the rich in my country.

MRS. ELLIS. He's quite right, Sophie. Not only something old but something so old that we're sick of it.

CROSSMAN. Why don't you give her a nice new check?

MRS. ELLIS. Only if I have to.

CONSTANCE *(On porch).* Nick, my neck is breaking —

NICK. All right. All finished for this morning. *(Turns the picture around so that* CONSTANCE *cannot see it.* SOPHIE *brings two cups of coffee to the porch.)*

CONSTANCE *(Collapsing in a chair).* Whew. *(Takes the coffee from* SOPHIE, *pats her arm.* SOPHIE *takes the other cup to* NICK.)

NICK.   You're the girl I want to paint. Change
your mind and we'll start today. Why not, Sophie?

(He is holding her hand.)

SOPHIE.   I am not pretty, Mr. Nicholas.

NICK.   You are better than pretty.

(CROSSMAN *comes out to the porch.* SOPHIE
disengages her hand, moves off.)

CROSSMAN *(Staring at* CONSTANCE*).*   My God, you
look awful, Constance. What did you get done up like
that for? You're poor enough not to have to pretend
you are poor.

NICK *(Laughing).*   Go way, Ned. You've got a
hangover. I know I have.

(NINA *comes down the steps, comes into the
room, says good morning to* MRS. ELLIS *who says
good morning to her. She pours herself a cup
of coffee. She is close enough to the porch to
hear what is said.)*

CONSTANCE.   You know, I waited up until twelve
o'clock for you both —

NICK.   We were late. We had a good get-together
last night. Like old times, wasn't it, Ned? *(To* CON-
STANCE*)* If you have the normal vanity you'd be pleased
at the amount of time we spent on you. Ned loosened
up and talked —

CROSSMAN.   I did? I thought that was you.

NICK *(Laughs).*   I knew you wouldn't remember
what you'd said — Don't regret it: did you good to
speak your heart out — for once.

CROSSMAN.   My heart, eh?

NICK. In a juke-box song called Constance.

CONSTANCE. What? I don't understand.

CROSSMAN *(Who has turned sharply, then decided to laugh).* Neither do I. The stage of not remembering, or speaking out my heart, will come in time, I am sorry to say. But I hope it hasn't come yet.

(As he turns to go out, LEON *appears in the hall with a bell and begins to ring the bell.)*

NINA *(A little timidly).* Good morning, Mr. Crossman.

CROSSMAN. Good morning, Mrs. Denery. I'm sorry you didn't join us last night — to hear me pour my heart out.

NINA. I'm never invited to the pouring of a heart.

CROSSMAN. I looked for you, but Nick said you had a headache.

NINA. Nick always says I have a headache when he doesn't want me to come along, or sees to it that I do have one.

MRS. ELLIS *(Gets up quickly).* All right, Leon. I'm ready. I haven't eaten since four this morning. *(Goes out. As she passes stairs, she shouts up)* Carrie! Frederick! I simply won't wait breakfast any longer.

(CROSSMAN follows her out.)

CONSTANCE *(Gets up).* Well, they seemed to have managed in the kitchen without me. I reckon I better change now. Where'd you get this dress, Nick?

NICK. Place on Dreyenen Street.

CONSTANCE. In a Negro store! You bought this dress in a Negro store! *(He looks at her and laughs)* I don't mean that. I mean Ned's right. You must have wanted to make me look just about as awful as — For some reason I don't understand. Nick, what *are* you doing? And why won't you let me see the portrait?

NICK. Haven't you yet figured out that Ned is jealous?

CONSTANCE. Jealous of what?

NICK. He's in love with you, girl. As much as he was when we were kids. You're all he talked about last night. How lonely he's been, how much he's wanted you, how often he asked you to marry him —

CONSTANCE. I just don't believe you. Ned never talks about himself. I just don't believe he said such things —

NICK. You know damn well he loves you and you know he's rotting away for you. He said last night —

CONSTANCE *(Prissy)*. Nick, if he did talk, and it's most out of character, I don't think I should hear what he said in confidence just to you.

NICK. Oh, run along, honey. You're pleased as punch. When you're not pretending to be genteel.

CONSTANCE *(Laughs)*. Genteel? How awful of me. Mama used to say gentility was the opposite of breeding and — *(She has started to move out of the room)* Did Ned say — er —

(Nick laughs, she laughs, and exits. NICK *begins to put away portrait and to fold easel as* NINA *puts down her coffee and comes out to the porch.)*

NICK *(Kisses her).* Morning, darling. (NINA *sits down, watches him)* What's the matter?

(LEON *appears with breakfast dishes. He serves* NICK *and* NINA *during the next few speeches.)*

NINA. Why have you done that? To Constance?

NICK. Done what? Tell her the truth?

NINA. How could you know it to be the truth? I don't believe Crossman talked to you —

NICK. Look, it makes her happy — and if I can get a little sense into her head it will make him happy. I don't have to have an affidavit to know what's going on in the human heart.

(He leans over, kisses her, sits down to eat his breakfast.)

NINA *(Laughs).* Oh, you are enjoying yourself so much here. I've seldom seen it this hog-wild. (LEON *exits)* You're on a rampage of good will. Makes me nervous for even the trees outside. But there's something impertinent about warning an oak tree. How should I do it?

NICK *(Laughs).* First tell me how to understand what you're talking about.

(They eat in silence for a minute.)

NINA. Are we staying much longer, Nick?

NICK. A few more days. The house officially closes this week, Constance says. The Ellises go tomorrow and the Griggses on Tuesday, I think. Just till I finish.

NINA. Finish what?

NICK *(Carefully).* The portrait, Nina.

(ROSE GRIGGS *comes down the stairs, carrying
a small overnight case. She is done up in a
pretty, too fussy, hat and a pretty, too fussy,
dress. She looks in the room, puts the case
down, comes hurrying out to the porch.*)

ROSE.   Oh, good morning. Sorry to interrupt. You
look so handsome together. *(Makes a gesture to* NICK
meaning "Could you come here?") Nick —

NICK *(Hospitable)*.   Come on out.

ROSE.   I'd rather. Could you —

NICK.   Come and join us.

ROSE *(Hesitantly)*.   Well, I wanted to tell *you* but
I don't want to worry Nina. You see —

NINA.   I'd go away, Mrs. Griggs, but I've been dis-
missed from so many meals lately that I'm getting
hungry.

ROSE *(Smiles to* NINA. *Speaks to* NICK*)*.   I called
him last night. Just like you advised. And I'm driving
right over now. He's the executor of my trust fund,
you know. He's very wise: I've got gilt-edged
securities.

NICK.   Who is this?

ROSE.   My brother, of course. Henry, like I told
you. *(To* NINA*)* It sounds so mysterious, but it isn't. He's
much older. You know he builds ships, I mean during
our wars. I'll tell him the whole story, Nick, and he'll
know what to do.

NICK *(Amused)*.   Of course he will.

ROSE.   I'm going to drive over to my doctor's.
He's going to wait for me on a hot Sunday. It'll be ex-

pensive — *(To* NINA) I had a heart murmur. They had to take me out of school for a year.

NINA. Recently?

(NICK *chokes back a laugh.*)

ROSE *(Giggles).* That's charming — "recently." *(To* NICK) There's so much I wanted to consult you about. I waited up for you last night, but — well. Should I do *just* as you told me yesterday?

NICK *(Who doesn't remember what he told her).* Sure.

ROSE. Everything?

NICK. Well —

NINA. I think, Mrs. Griggs, you'll have to remind Nick what he told you. Yesterday is a long time ago when you have so many ladies to attend to —

ROSE *(As* NICK *laughs).* I shouldn't have brought it up like this. Oh, Mrs. Denery, you might as well know: it's about a divorce, and Nick has been most kind.

NINA. I am sure of it.

ROSE. Just one more thing. What should I do about our boys? Should I telephone them or let Henry? One of our sons works on the atom bomb, you know. He's the religious one and it will be traumatic for him. What do you think, Nick?

NINA *(Gets up quickly, trying not to laugh, moves away).* Goodness.

NICK. I think you should go and have your breakfast. It's my firm belief that women only look well in hats after they've eaten.

Rose *(To* Nick, *softly, secretly).*   And I'm going to just *make* Henry commission the portrait — and for the very good price that he can afford to pay. You remember though that I told you she can't take the braces off her teeth for another six months.

Nick *(Laughs).*   Go along now, my dear.

Rose *(Pleased).*   Thank you for all you've done. And forgive me, Nina. I'll be back tonight, Nick, before you go to bed because you'll want to know how everything turns out.

(She exits through room. Nina *stands without speaking.)*

Nick *(Looks up at her).*   There was a day when we would have laughed together about this. Don't you have fun any more?

Nina.   I don't think so.

Nick.   She's quite nice, really. And very funny.

Nina.   I suppose it's all right to flirt with, or to charm, women and men and children and animals but nowadays it seems to me you include books-in-vellum and sirloin steaks, red squirrels and lamp shades.

Nick *(Smiles).*   Are you crazy? Flirt with that silly woman? Come and eat your breakfast, Nina. I've had enough seriousness where none is due.

(Through this speech, Carrie *has come down the steps. She meets* Sophie *who is going through the hall to the dining room.* Sophie *is carrying a tray.)*

Carrie.   Good morning, dear. Is Frederick in the dining room?

SOPHIE.   No. He has not come down as yet.
(She goes on past. CARRIE *comes into the room,
continues on to the porch.)*

CARRIE *(To* NICK *and* NINA*).*   Good morning. Your
maid said you wanted to see me, Nick.

NICK *(Hesitantly).*   Carrie, I hesitated all day yesterday. I told myself perhaps you knew, but maybe,
just maybe, you didn't.

NINA *(Laughs).*   Oh, it sounds so serious.

CARRIE *(Smiles).*   It does indeed.

NICK *(Carefully).*   Don't you know that man's
reputation, Carrie? You can't travel around Europe
with him.

CARRIE.   Travel around Europe with *him?* I'm
going to Europe with Frederick. *(Then sharply, as she
sees his face)* What do you mean, Nick?

NICK.   I —

*(*SOPHIE *comes into room, goes out to porch.
During next speeches, she pours coffee.)*

CARRIE.   Please tell me.

NICK.   I saw Frederick in the travel agency yesterday with a man I once met in Europe. Not the sort of
man you'd expect to see Frederick with.

CARRIE.   Are you talking about Mr. Payson?

NICK.   Yes, I am. Well, I waited until they left
the travel place and then I went in.

NINA.   Why did you go in?

NICK.   Luther hadn't seen me since we were kids
and we got to talking. He said he had booked your
passage on the *Elizabeth* and now he had another

for Mr. Payson and Fred had just paid for it —
(CARRIE *gets up, turns sharply, does not speak.*)
I didn't know whether you knew, Carrie, or if I should
tell you —

CARRIE.   I didn't know. I thank you for telling me.
(After a second, she turns) What did you mean, Nick,
when you asked me if I knew Payson's reputation? I
don't like to press you for gossip, but —

NINA.   He didn't mean anything, Mrs. Ellis —

NICK.   Oh, look here, Nina, you know he's part
of Count Denna's set, and on the nasty fringe of
that.

(SOPHIE, *very quietly, leaves the porch.*)

CARRIE.   What does that mean: Count Denna's
set and the nasty fringe of that?

NINA *(Quickly)*.   It means very little. The Count
is a foolish old man who gives large parties —

NICK *(To NINA)*.   Would you want your young
son with such people at such parties?

NINA *(Angrily)*.   I have no son. And I don't know:
perhaps I would have wanted only to leave him alone —

CARRIE *(Gently)*.   All people who have no children
think that, Mrs. Denery. But it just isn't true. *(To
NICK)* I don't know much about Mr. Payson but I've
been worried for a long time that he's taken Frederick
in. Frederick admires his writing, and — Yet I know so
little about him. He stayed with us a few weeks in town
last winter. He'd just come back from Europe then —

NICK.   He'd just come back from a filthy little
scandal in Rome. It was all over the papers.

NINA. You don't know it was true.

CARRIE. What kind of scandal? *(No answer. Softly)* Please help me. I don't understand.

NICK *(Gets up)*. Look, Carrie, there's nothing to understand. The guy is just no good. That's all you need to know. He's nobody to travel around Europe with.

CARRIE. How could Fred have — *(She hesitates for a minute)* It was kind and friendly of you to tell me. I am grateful to you both.

(She goes slowly across the room and into the hall toward the dining room. There is a long pause: NICK takes a sip of coffee, looks around at NINA.)

NICK. What would you have done?

NINA *(Idly)*. I don't know. Have you ever tried leaving things alone?

NICK. I like Carrie. She doesn't know what the hell it's all about — and the chances are the boy doesn't either. I'm sorry for them. Aren't you? *(When she doesn't answer)* What's the matter, Nina?

NINA. I can smell it: it's all around us. The flower-like odor right before it becomes troublesome and heavy. It travels ahead of you, Nick, whenever you get most helpful, most loving and most lovable. Down through the years it runs ahead of us — I smell it — and I want to leave.

NICK *(Pleasantly)*. I think maybe you're one of the few neurotics in the world who didn't marry a neurotic. I wonder how that happened?

NINA. *I want to leave.*

NICK *(Sharply).*   Then leave.

NINA *(After a second).*   You won't come?

NICK.   I told you: we'll go Friday. If you want to go before, then go. But stop talking about it, Nina. Or we'll be in for one of your long farewells — and long returns. I don't think I can stand another. Spare yourself, darling. You pay so heavy, inside. *(Comes to her, puts his arms around her)* Friday, then. And in the meantime, gentle down to the pretty lady you truly are.

> *(He kisses her. Exits.)*
>
> *(NINA stands quietly for a minute. SOPHIE comes onto the porch, begins to gather the dishes.)*

SOPHIE *(Gently).*   Would you like something, Mrs. Denery?

NINA *(Softly).*   No, thank you.

> *(She moves off, through the room and toward the staircase. As she starts up the stairs, FREDERICK comes down.)*

FREDERICK.   Good morning.

NINA.   Good morning, Mr. Ellis. *(Stops as if she wanted to tell him something)* I — er. Good morning.

> *(She goes up as SOPHIE, who has heard their voices, leaves the dishes and comes quickly into the room.)*

SOPHIE *(Calling into the hall).*   Fred. Fred. *(He comes in. Shyly)* Would you like to have your breakfast on the kitchen porch?

FREDERICK.   Sure. Why?

SOPHIE. Your mother is — er — *(Points toward dining room)* She has found out that — Come.

FREDERICK. Denery told her he saw me in the travel agency. I was sure he would. There's nothing to worry about. I intended to tell her this morning.

SOPHIE. But perhaps it would be more wise —

FREDERICK *(Smiles to her)*. We'll be leaving here tomorrow and for Europe on the sixteenth. You and I won't see each other for six months. Sophie, you're sure you feel all right about my going?

SOPHIE *(Quickly)*. Oh, I do.

FREDERICK. We will visit your mother. And —

SOPHIE *(Very quickly)*. No, no, please do not do that. I have not written to her about us —

FREDERICK. Oh.

SOPHIE. You see, we have as yet no date of time, or —

FREDERICK *(Smiles)*. I don't think you want a date of time, Sophie. And you don't have to be ashamed of wishing you could find another way. But if there isn't any other way for you, then I'll be just as good to you as I know how. And I know you will be to me.

SOPHIE. You are a kind man. And I will also be kind, I hope.

FREDERICK. It isn't any deal for you. You are a girl who should love, and will one day, of course.

SOPHIE *(Puts her hand up to her mouth)*. Shssh. Such things should not be said. *(Cheerfully)* It will be nice in your house with you, and I will be grateful for it.

FREDERICK. I have no house, Sophie. People like me never have their own house, so-to-speak.

SOPHIE. Never mind. Whatever house. It will be nice. We will make it so.

(*He smiles, pats her arm.*)

FREDERICK. Everybody in the dining room? (*She nods. He starts for hall*) Might as well face it out.

SOPHIE. I would not. No, I would not. All of you face out too much. Every act of life should not be of such importance —

FREDERICK (*Calling into dining room*). Mother. (SOPHIE *shrugs, smiles, shakes her head, and exits.* FREDERICK *comes back into room, pours himself a cup of coffee. After a minute,* CARRIE *appears. She comes into the room obviously very disturbed. But she does not speak.*) There's nothing to be so upset about.

CARRIE (*After a pause*). You think that, really?

(MRS. ELLIS *appears in the hall.*)

FREDERICK. We've going to have a companion. That's all. We know nothing of traveling and Payson knows all of Europe.

MRS. ELLIS. Of course. You're lucky to get Mr. Payson to come along.

(*Both of them turn to look at her.*)

FREDERICK (*After a second, to* CARRIE). What is it, Mother?

CARRIE. I can't say it. It's shocking of you to take along a guest without consulting me. You and I have planned this trip for three years and —

FREDERICK. I didn't consult you because the idea came up quickly and Payson had to get his ticket before the travel office closed for the week end —

CARRIE. *Payson* had to get *his* ticket?

FREDERICK. I thought you'd given up going through my checkbooks.

CARRIE. *Please don't speak that way to me. (Pause, quietly, delicately)* We are not going to Europe.

FREDERICK *(After a second, quietly).* I am.

CARRIE. We are not going, Fred. We are not going.

MRS. ELLIS. Your mother's feelings are hurt. She had looked forward to being alone with you. Of course.

FREDERICK *(Uncomfortably).* We'll still be together.

CARRIE *(To Mrs. Ellis).* I don't wish to be interpreted, Mother. *(To* FREDERICK*)* There's no sense talking about it: we'll go another time.

FREDERICK *(Laughs, unpleasantly).* Will you stop acting as if you're taking me back to school? I will be disappointed if you don't wish to come with me but I am sailing on the sixteenth. *(Then, quietly)* I've never had much fun. Never seen the things I wished to see, never met the people I wanted to meet or been the places where I could. There are wonderful things to see and to learn about and to try to understand. We're lucky to have somebody who knows about them and who is willing to have *us* tag along. *I'm* not much to drag around — *(Softly)* I'll come back, and you can take up my life again. Six months isn't much to ask.

MRS. ELLIS. Six months? Sad to ask so little.

CARRIE (*As if she recognized a tone of voice*). Mother, please. I —

MRS. ELLIS. Perhaps you won't want to come back at all? I wouldn't blame you.

CARRIE (*Nervously*). Fred, don't make a decision now. Promise me you'll think about it until tomorrow and then we'll talk quietly and —

MRS. ELLIS (*To* FREDERICK). Don't make bargains with your mother. Everything always ends that way between you. I advise you to go now, or stay.

FREDERICK. I am going. There is nothing to think about. I'm going.

(*He turns and exits, goes up staircase. There is a pause.*)

CARRIE (*Angry*). You always do that, Mother. You always arrange to come out his friend and make me his enemy. You've been amusing yourself that way all his life.

MRS. ELLIS. There's no time for all that, Carrie. I warned you to say and do nothing. I told you to make the best of it and go along with them.

CARRIE (*Softly*). How could I do that? That man is a scoundrel and Fred doesn't know it, and won't believe it. What am I to do now?

MRS. ELLIS. You're to go upstairs and say that you are reconciled to his leaving without you but that Frederick is to make clear to his guest that his ten thousand a year ends today and will not begin again. Tell him you've decided young people have a happier time in Europe without American money —

CARRIE *(Sharply).* I couldn't do that. He'd hate me for it. Maybe we'd better let him go, and perhaps I can join him later. Time will — *(Sees* MRS. ELLIS's *face)* I will not cut off his allowance.

MRS. ELLIS. I didn't know it was you who wrote the check.

CARRIE *(With dignity).* Are you quite sure you wish to speak this way?

MRS. ELLIS. Relatively sure.

CARRIE. Then I will say as sharply that the money is his father's money, and not yours to threaten him, or deprive him, in any proper sense.

MRS. ELLIS. In any *proper* sense. There is no morality to money, Carrie, and very immoral of you to think so.

CARRIE. If you stop his allowance, Mother, I will simply send him mine.

MRS. ELLIS. Then I won't give you yours. (CARRIE *turns sharply, as if she were deeply shocked.* MRS. ELLIS *now speaks, gently)* Yes, old people are often harsh, Carrie, when they control the purse. You'll see, when your day comes. And then, too, one comes to be bored with those who fool themselves. I say to myself — one should have power, or give it over. But if one keeps it, it might as well be used, with as little mealymouthness as possible. Go up now, and press him hard, and do it straight. (CARRIE *turns slowly to exit)* Tell yourself you're doing it for his own good.

CARRIE *(Softly)*.   I wouldn't be doing it otherwise.

MRS. ELLIS.   Perhaps. Perhaps not. Doesn't really matter. *(Laughs, amused)* I'm off to church now. You can skip church today, Carrie.

CARRIE.   Thank you for the dispensation.
(She begins to move off toward hall and toward stairs as ROSE *comes from the direction of the dining room and into the room.)*

MRS. ELLIS *(To* CARRIE, *as* CARRIE *moves off)*. Quite all right. You have God's work to do. *(She turns to watch* ROSE *who is elaborately settling herself in a chair as if she were arranging for a scene — which is what she is doing)* What are you doing, Mrs. Griggs? *(*ROSE *nervously points to left window.* MRS. ELLIS *looks toward it, watches* ROSE *fix her face)* Is it Robert Taylor you're expecting or Vice-President Barkley? *(*GRIGGS *comes in from the left windows. He has on riding pants and an old shirt)* Oh.

GRIGGS *(To them both)*.   Good morning.

MRS. ELLIS.   Your wife's getting ready to flirt. You'd be safer in church with me.
(She exits as GRIGGS *laughs. He goes to coffee urn.)*

ROSE *(Meaning* MRS. ELLIS*)*. Nasty old thing. *(Then)* I'm driving over to see him. I'm sorry I had to make such a decision, but I felt it was necessary now.

GRIGGS.   Are you talking about your brother?

ROSE.   Yes, of course. Now, I know it will be bad for you, Ben, but since *you're* being so stubborn, I didn't know what else to do.

GRIGGS. I think you should see Henry.

ROSE. But he's going to be very, very angry, Ben. And you know how much influence he has in Washington.

GRIGGS *(Turns, carefully)*. Tell him to use his influence. And tell him to go to hell.

ROSE *(Giggles)*. On a Sunday?

GRIGGS *(Gently)*. Rose, no years will make you serious.

ROSE. You used to like me that way.

GRIGGS. So you always wanted to believe.

ROSE. How can I just walk into Henry's happy house and say Ben wants a divorce, and I don't even know the reason. I *ask* him and I *ask* him but he says there is no reason —

GRIGGS. I never said there was no reason. But it isn't the reason that you like, or will accept. If I were in love with another woman you'd rather enjoy that. And certainly Henry would.

ROSE. It would at least be human. And I am not convinced it isn't so. I've done a good deal of thinking about it, and I've just about decided it's why you stayed in Europe so long.

GRIGGS. I didn't arrange World War II and don't listen to the rumors that I did.

ROSE. He said it at the time. He said he had known a good many professional soldiers but nobody had managed to make so much fuss about the war as you did, or to stay away so long. Henry said that.

GRIGGS. I guessed it was Henry who said that.

ROSE (*Laughs*).   But you didn't guess that it was Henry who got you the last promotion.

GRIGGS.   Rose, stop that. You're lying. You always do it about now. (*Turns to her*) Give Henry this reason: tell him my wife's too young for me. For Henry's simple mind, a simple reason.

ROSE.   I've wanted to stay young, I've —

GRIGGS.   You've done more than stay young: you've stayed a child.

ROSE.   What about your mother, Ben, have you thought of her? It would kill her —

GRIGGS.   She's been dead sixteen years. Do you think this will kill her?

ROSE.   You know what I mean. She loved me and she was happy for our marriage.

GRIGGS.   No, she didn't. She warned me not to marry — (*With feeling*) I began my life with a serious woman. I doubt if any man gets over that, or ever really wants any other kind of woman.

ROSE.   *Your mother loved me.* You have no right to malign the dead. I say she loved me, I know she did.

GRIGGS (*Wearily*).   What difference does it make?

ROSE.   You never think anybody loves me. Quite a few men have found me attractive —

GRIGGS (*Quickly*).   And many more will, my dear.

ROSE.   I always knew in the end I would have to tell you although I haven't seen him since you came home. That I promise you. I told him you were a war hero with a glorious record and he said he wouldn't either any longer —

GRIGGS *(Who is at the left window).* Henry's chauffeur is outside, Rose.

ROSE.   He was very, very, very, very much in love with me while he was at the Pentagon.

GRIGGS.   Good place to be in love. The car is outside, Rose.

ROSE.   Even after we both knew it, he kept on saying that you didn't make love to a friend, more than a friend's, wife.

GRIGGS *(Gently).*   Rose, don't let's talk this way.

ROSE.   Does it hurt you? Well, you've hurt me enough. The third time you went to Europe was when it really began, maybe the second. Because I, too, wanted affection.

GRIGGS *(Gently).*   I can understand that.

. ROSE.   Ask me who it was. Ask me, Ben, and I will tell you. *(No answer)* Just ask me.

GRIGGS.   No, I won't do that, Rose.

ROSE.   Remember when the roses came from Teheran, I mean wired from Teheran, last birthday? That's who sent them. You didn't even like Teheran. You said it was filthy and the people downtrodden. But he sent roses.

GRIGGS.   He sounds like the right man. Go to him, Rose, the flying time is nothing now.

ROSE *(Angrily).*   You just stop being nasty. *(Then)* And now I am going to tell you who it is.

GRIGGS *(Begins to move toward door, as if he were backing away from her).*   Please, Rose. We have had so many years of this — Please. *(As she is closer to him)*

Do I have to tell you that I don't care who it is?

ROSE *(She begins to move on him).* I'd like to whisper it. I knew if I ever told you I'd have to whisper it. *(He begins now really to back away)* Ben, you come right here. Ben stand still. *(He starts to laugh)* Stop that laughing. *(Very loudly, very close to him)* It was your cousin, Ralph Sommers. There. *(She turns away)* There. You won't ever speak with him about it?

GRIGGS. You can be sure of that.

ROSE *(Outside an automobile horn is sounded).* Oh, I'm late. I can't talk any more now, Ben. *(She starts for door, stops)* What am I going to tell Henry? Anyway, you know Henry isn't going to allow me to give you a divorce. You know that, Ben. *(Carefully)* And therefore I won't be able to do what you want, and the whole day is just wasted. Please tell me not to go, Ben.

GRIGGS *(As if he has held on to himself long enough).* Tell Henry that I want a divorce. But in any case I am going away. I am leaving. That is all that matters to me or need matter to you or him. I would prefer a divorce. But I am going, whatever you and Henry decide. Understand that, Rose, the time has come to understand it.

ROSE *(Gently, smiling).* I am going to try, dear. Really I am. It's evidently important to you.

(She exits through hall. GRIGGS *sits down as if he were very tired. A minute later,* CROSS-MAN *comes from the direction of the dining room, carrying the Sunday papers. He looks*

at BEN, *goes to him, hands him the front page.*
BEN *takes it, nods, sits holding it.* CROSSMAN
*crosses to a chair, sits down, begins to read the
comic section. A second later,* NINA *comes
down the stairs, comes into the room, starts to
speak to* BEN *and* CROSSMAN, *changes her mind
and sits down. Then* CONSTANCE, *in an old-
fashioned flowered hat and carrying a large
palmetto fan, comes through the hall and into
the room.)*

CONSTANCE. I'm off to church. Anybody want
anything just ring for Leon or Sophie. *(Bravely)* Want
to come to church with me, Ned? *(He peers over his
paper, amazed)* All right. I just thought — Well, Nick
told us that you told him last night —

CROSSMAN *(Laughs)*. I think perhaps I shall never
again go out at night.

CONSTANCE. Oh, it's good for all of us to confide
in somebody — *(She becomes conscious of* NINA *and*
GRIGGS, *smiles awkwardly and then with great determi-
nation leans over and kisses* CROSSMAN) Good-by, darling.

*(Surprised, he gets up, stands watching her
leave the room. Then he sits down, staring
ahead.)*

NINA *(After a minute, hesitantly)*. I've got a car
and a full picnic basket and a cold bottle of wine.
Would you — *(Turning to* CROSSMAN *and then to*
GRIGGS) like to come along? I don't know where to go,
but —

CROSSMAN.   Got enough in your picnic basket for lunch *and* dinner?

NINA *(Smiles)*.   I think so.

CROSSMAN.   Got a mandolin?

NINA *(Smiles)*.   No. Does that rule me out?

CROSSMAN.   Almost. But we'll make do. The General whistles very well.

GRIGGS *(Smiles, gets up)*.   Is one bottle of wine enough on a Sunday?

NINA *(Laughs as she goes toward hall)*.   Not for the pure in heart. I'll get five or six more.

(GRIGGS follows her out through hall. CROSSMAN gets up, folds the comic section, puts it under his arm, exits through hall. As he exits, SOPHIE comes on the porch. She begins to pile the breakfast dishes on a tray. She sees a half-used roll and a piece of bacon, fixes it for herself, goes out carrying the tray and chewing on the roll as the curtain falls.)

CURTAIN

ACT TWO

Scene Two

SCENE:
THE SAME. *Nine-thirty that evening.*

AT RISE:
NICK *is lying on the couch. Next to him, on the floor, is an empty champagne glass. On the table, in a silver cooler, is a bottle of champagne.* CONSTANCE *is sitting at the table playing solitaire and humming to the record on the phonograph. On the porch,* SOPHIE *is reading to* MRS. MARY ELLIS.

NICK *(Looks up from couch to* CONSTANCE, *irritably).* Please don't hum.

CONSTANCE. Sorry. I always like that so much, I —

NICK. And please don't talk. Mozart doesn't need it.

CONSTANCE. Haydn.

NICK. Mozart.

CONSTANCE *(Tartly).* I'm sorry but it's Haydn.

NICK. You know damn well I know what I'm talking about.

CONSTANCE. You don't know what you're talking about. Go look.

NICK *(Gets up, picks up his glass, goes to phonograph, shuts it off, looks down, turns away annoyed, picks up a champagne bottle, pours himself a drink, then brings the bottle to* CONSTANCE*).* Ready for another?

CONSTANCE. I haven't finished this.

(NICK *carries the bottle out to the porch.*)

MRS. ELLIS *(Looks up at him).* For the fourth time, we don't want any. Please go away. We're having a nice time. We're in the part I like best.

NICK. A nice time? Will I think such a time is a nice time when I am your age? I suppose so.

MRS. ELLIS. No, Mr. Denery. If you haven't learned to read at your age, you won't learn at mine.

NICK *(Laughs, pats her shoulder).* Never mind, I like you.

MRS. ELLIS. You must be damn hard up. People seldom like those who don't like them.

NICK *(Pleased).* You haven't forgotten how to flirt. Come on inside and talk to me. My wife disappears, everybody disappears — *(Stretches)* I'm bored, I'm bored.

MRS. ELLIS. And that's a state of sin, isn't it?

NICK. Unfortunately, it isn't. I've always said I can stand any pain, any trouble — but not boredom.

MRS. ELLIS. My advice is to try something intellectual for a change. Sit down with your champagne —

on which you've been chewing since early afternoon —
and try to make a paper hat out of the newspaper or get
yourself a nice long piece of string.

NICK *(Goes to* SOPHIE*).*   Sophie, come in and dance
with me.

MRS. ELLIS *(Calls in).*   Constance, whistle for Mr.
Denery, please.

NICK *(To* SOPHIE*).*   You don't want to sit here and
read to Mrs. Ellis.

SOPHIE.   Yes, sir, I do. I enjoy the adventures of
Odysseus. And the dollar an hour Mrs. Ellis pays me
for reading to her.

NICK *(Laughs, as* MRS. ELLIS *laughs).*   Give you two
dollars an hour to dance with me.

MRS. ELLIS.   It's not nearly enough, Sophie.

NICK *(Pats* MRS. ELLIS*).*   You're a corrupter of
youth — you steal the best hours.

MRS. ELLIS *(Shakes his hand off her shoulder).*
And you're a toucher: you constantly touch people or
lean on them. Little moments of sensuality. One should
have sensuality whole or not at all. Don't you find
pecking at it ungratifying? There are many of you: the
touchers and the leaners. All since the depression, is my
theory.

NICK *(Laughs, pats her again).*   You must have
been quite a girl in your day.

MRS. ELLIS.   I wasn't. I wasn't at all. (NICK *wanders into the room.* MRS. ELLIS *speaks to* SOPHIE) I was
too good for those who wanted me and not good enough
for those I wanted. Like Frederick, Sophie. Life can

be hard for such people and they seldom understand
why and end bitter and confused.

SOPHIE. I know.

MRS. ELLIS. Do you? Frederick is a nice boy,
Sophie — and that is all. But that's more than most, and
precious in a small way.

SOPHIE. Yes, I think so.

(MRS. ELLIS *smiles, pats her hand;* SOPHIE *begins again to read.*)

NICK (*Near the phonograph, to* CONSTANCE).
Dance with me?

CONSTANCE. I don't know how any more.

NICK (*Turns away from the phonograph*). Has it
been wise, Constance, to lose all the graces in the service
of this house?

CONSTANCE. Do you think I wanted it that way?

NICK. I'm not sure you didn't. You could have
married Ned, instead of dangling him around, the way
you've done.

CONSTANCE. Ned has come here each summer
because, well, because I guess this is about the only home
he has. I loved Ned and honored him, but — I just
wasn't in love with him when we were young. You know
that, and you'd have been the first to tell me that you
can't marry unless you're in love — (*He begins to laugh*)
What are you laughing at?

NICK. "Can't marry unless you're in love." What
do you think the rest of us did? I was in love with you.
I've never been in love again.

CONSTANCE (*Very sharply*). I don't want you to

talk to me that way. And I don't believe you. You fell in love with Nina and that's why you didn't come back — *(Desperately)* You're *very* much in love with Nina. Then and now. Then —

NICK.   Have it your way. What are you so angry about? Want to know something: I've never been angry in my life. *(Turns to her, smiles)* In the end, we wouldn't have worked out. You're a good woman and I am not a good man.

CONSTANCE.   Well, whatever the reason, things turned out for the best. *(Carefully)* About Ned. What did he say last night? I mean did he really talk about me?

NICK *(Expansively)*.   He said he loved you and wanted you and had wasted his life loving you and wanting you. And that he wasn't coming here any more. This is his last summer in this house.

CONSTANCE *(She turns, pained, startled)*.   His last summer? He said that? He really said it was his last summer —

     (CARRIE *comes quickly into the room.*)

CARRIE.   Has Fred come back?

NICK *(To her)*.   Well, where have *you* been? Come and have a drink and talk to me.

     (He moves to pour her a drink as she crosses to the porch.)

CARRIE *(Softly, to* MRS. ELLIS*)*.   I've been everywhere. Everywhere possible. I even forced myself to call on Mr. Payson.

MRS. ELLIS.   And what did he say?

CARRIE.   That Fred came in to see him after he

left here this morning, stayed a few minutes, no more, and he hasn't seen him since.

MRS. ELLIS.   Ah, that's good.

CARRIE.   What's good about it? It means we don't know where he's been since ten this morning. *(Softly, as she sits down)* I don't know what else to do or where else to look. What should I do? Shall I call the police, what else is there to do?

MRS. ELLIS.   Nothing.

CARRIE.   How can I do nothing? You shouldn't have made me threaten him. We were wrong. It wasn't important that he wanted to go to Europe with a man his own age. What harm was there in it?

MRS. ELLIS.   All his life you've been plucking him this way and plucking him that. Do what you like. Call the police.

NICK *(Who has come to the door carrying a glass for* CARRIE. *He hears the last few speeches; gently).*   Can I do anything, Carrie?

CARRIE.   I don't know, Nick. I only found one person who had seen him, down by the water —

NICK.   Is he — would he have — is that what you're thinking, Carrie?

CARRIE.   I'm afraid, I'm afraid.

NICK *(Quickly, the kind of efficiency that comes with liquor and boredom).*   Then come on, Carrie. You must go to the police right away. I'll get a boat. Tell the police to follow along. Right away.

*(*CARRIE *gets up. Starts toward Nick.* SOPHIE *gets up.)*

SOPHIE *(Angrily, in French, to* NICK*)*. Do not enjoy the excitement so much. Stop being a fool.

NICK *(Amazed)*. What?

SOPHIE *(In German)*. I said don't enjoy yourself so much. Mind your business.

CARRIE. What? What is it, Sophie?

SOPHIE *(To* CARRIE*)*. Frederick is in the cove down by the dock. He has been there all day.

NICK *(To* SOPHIE*)*. You said I was a fool. I don't like such words, Sophie. I don't.

CARRIE *(Carefully, to* SOPHIE*)*. You've let me go running about all day, frantic with terror —

SOPHIE. He wanted to be alone, Mrs. Ellis. That is not so terrible a thing to want.

CARRIE. How dare you take this on yourself? How dare you —

MRS. ELLIS. I hope this is not a sample of you as a mother-in-law.

SOPHIE *(Gently, to* CARRIE*)*. He will return, Mrs. Ellis. Leave him alone.

NICK *(Softly)*. Sophie, I think you owe me an apology. You are by way of being a rather sharp little girl underneath all that shyness, aren't you? I'm waiting. *(No answer)* I'm waiting.

MRS. ELLIS. Well, wait outside, will you?

(He stares at her, turns, goes in the room.)

NICK *(Very hurt, to* CONSTANCE*)*. I don't think I like it around here, Constance. No, I don't like it.

(He goes out left windows as CONSTANCE *stares at him.)*

CARRIE.   Since Frederick has confided in you, Sophie, perhaps you should go to him.

SOPHIE.   He has not confided in me. Sometimes his troubles are his own.

(She gets up, walks through room, sits down near CONSTANCE, *who looks at her curiously. On the porch,* MRS. ELLIS *leans over and whispers to* CARRIE.*)*

CARRIE.   Not tonight.

MRS. ELLIS.   Why not tonight? We'll be leaving in the morning.

CARRIE.   Because I've changed my mind. I think it best now that we let him go to Europe.

MRS. ELLIS *(Gets up).*   He will not want to go to Europe. Haven't you understood that much?

CARRIE *(Hesitantly).*   How do you know what he wants or feels —

MRS. ELLIS.   I know. *(She comes into room, sits near* CONSTANCE *and* SOPHIE. *After a second* CARRIE *follows her in, stands near them)* Sophie, I think a decision had best be made now. There should be no further postponement.

CARRIE *(Very nervous).*   This isn't the time. Fred will be angry —

MRS. ELLIS *(To* SOPHIE*).*   I don't want to push you, child, but nothing will change, nothing. I know you've wanted to wait, and so did Frederick, both of you hoping that maybe — But it will all be the same a year from now. Miracles don't happen. I'm telling you the truth, Sophie.

SOPHIE. Yes, Mrs. Ellis, and I agree with you. Nothing will change. If Frederick is willing for an early marriage then I am also willing.

CONSTANCE. Is this the way it's been? *Willing* to marry, *willing* to *marry* —

SOPHIE *(Looks at her)*. I do not use the correct word?

CONSTANCE *(To* MRS. ELLIS *and* CARRIE*)*. If that's the way it is, then I am not willing. I thought it was two young people who — who — who loved each other. I didn't ever understand it, and I didn't ask questions, but — Willing to get married. What have you been thinking of, why — *(Sharply, hurt)* What kind of unpleasant thing has this been?

CARRIE. I — I know. I can't —

MRS. ELLIS *(To* CONSTANCE *and* CARRIE*)*. Why don't you take each other by the hand and go outside and gather in the dew?

SOPHIE. I think Aunt Constance is sad that we do not speak of it in the romantic words of love.

CONSTANCE. Yes, I am. And shocked. When Carrie first talked to me about the marriage, I asked you immediately and you told me you were in love —

SOPHIE. I never told you that, Aunt Constance.

CONSTANCE. I don't remember your exact words but of course I understood — You mean you and Frederick have never been in love? Why? Then why have you —

SOPHIE. Aunt Constance, I do not wish to go on with my life as it has been. I have not been happy, and

I cannot continue here. I cannot be what you have wished me to be, and I do not want the world you want for me. It is too late —

CONSTANCE *(Softly)*. Too late? You were thirteen years old when you came here. I've tried to give you everything —

SOPHIE. I came from another world and in that world thirteen is not young. I know what you have tried to give me, and I am grateful. But it has been a foolish waste for us both.

CONSTANCE *(Softly)*. Were you happy at home, Sophie?

SOPHIE. I did not think in such words.

CONSTANCE. Please tell me.

SOPHIE. I was comfortable with myself, if that is what you mean, and I am no longer.

CONSTANCE *(Gently, takes her hand)*. I have been so wrong. And so careless in not seeing it. Do you want to go home now?

SOPHIE. No. My mother cannot — Well, it is not that easy. I do not — *(As if it were painful)* I do not wish to go home now.

CONSTANCE *(Puzzled)*. It's perfectly simple for you to go home. Why, why isn't it?

SOPHIE. I do not want to say, Aunt Constance. I do not want to. *(With feeling)* Please do not talk of it any more. Please allow me to do what I wish to do, and know is best for me. *(Smiles)* And don't look such a way. Frederick and I will have a nice life, we will make it so. *(Goes out.)*

CARRIE *(Sharply)*.   Don't be too disturbed, Constance. I have decided that Frederick should go to Europe and this time I am not going to allow any interference of any kind.

(FREDERICK *appears in the hall, comes into the room.*)

FREDERICK.   I'm not going to Europe, Mother.

CARRIE *(Turns to him)*.   I have had a bad day. And I have thought of many things. I was mistaken and you were right. You must go wherever you want — however you want to go.

FREDERICK.   I am not going, Mother. Payson made that very clear to me this morning.

MRS. ELLIS.   Don't, Frederick. It's not necessary. I know.

FREDERICK.   But evidently Mother doesn't. . . . Payson made it clear to me that I was not wanted and never had been unless I supplied the money.

(CONSTANCE *gets up, moves off to the porch.*)

CARRIE *(After a second)*.   I — Er — I don't believe he meant that. You just tell him that it's all been a mistake and there will certainly be money for the trip. Just go right back and say that, Frederick —

FREDERICK *(Very sharply)*.   Mother! I don't want to see him again! Ever.

CARRIE.   You often imagine people don't like you for yourself. *I'll* go and tell Mr. Payson that it's all fixed now —

MRS. ELLIS.   Carrie, you're an ass. *(To* FREDERICK*)* But I hope you haven't wasted today feeling bitter about

Mr. Payson. You have no right to bitterness. No right
at all. Why shouldn't Mr. Payson have wanted your
money, though I must say he seems to have been rather
boorish about not getting it. People like us should pay
for the interest of people like him. Why should they
want us otherwise? I don't believe he ever pretended to
feel anything else about you.

FREDERICK *(Softly)*.   No, he never pretended.

MRS. ELLIS.   Then understand that you've been
the fool, and not he the villain. Take next week to be
sad: a week's long enough to be sad in, if it's true sad-
ness. Plenty long enough.

FREDERICK *(Smiles)*.   All right, Grandma. I'll take
a week.

(SOPHIE *appears at the hall door.*)

SOPHIE *(To* FREDERICK*)*.   You have had no dinner?
(Puts out her hand) Then come. I have made a tray for
you.

*(He turns, goes to her, takes her hand, goes
out.)*

MRS. ELLIS *(Gets up, looks at* CARRIE*)*.   Are you going to interfere this time, Carrie? *(No answer. Gently)*
I hope not.

(She goes out. CARRIE *stands for a minute near
the porch. Then she goes out to* CONSTANCE.*)*

CARRIE.   I don't like it either.

CONSTANCE *(Wearily)*.   Whole thing sounds like
the sale of a shore-front property. I don't know. Seems
to me I've been so mixed up about so much. Well,
maybe you all know what you're doing.

CARRIE.   I don't know what I'm doing.

CONSTANCE.   Why did you want the marriage, Carrie? I mean a month ago when you spoke to me —

CARRIE.   I don't even know that.

CONSTANCE.   You always seem so clear about everything. And so strong. Even when we were girls. I envied you that, Carrie, and wanted to be like you.

CARRIE *(Laughs).*   Clear and strong? I wish I could tell you what I've missed and what I've wanted. Don't envy me, Con.

(She exits toward hall and staircase. As she does, NICK *comes in. He is now a little more drunk than when he went out.)*

NICK.   Come on out, Carrie. It's wonderful night. Take you for a sail.

CARRIE *(Laughs).*   Good night, Nick.

NICK *(As she goes up steps).*   I'm lonely, Carrie. I wouldn't leave you if you were lonely. *(When she doesn't answer, he goes into room, looks around, sees* CONSTANCE *sitting on the porch, goes over, stands in the door looking out. After a second)* I wish I wanted to go to bed with you, Con. I just can't want to. I don't know why. I just don't want it.

CONSTANCE *(Very sharply).*   Stop talking that way. You've had too much to drink.

(She gets up, comes into room. He grabs her arm.)

NICK.   Now you're angry again. *(Puts his arms around her)* I'll sing you a lullaby. Will you like that?

CONSTANCE.   Look, Nick, you've been rather a trial tonight. Do go to bed.

NICK.   I'm not going to bed.   I'm lonely. I'm —

(The phone rings. CONSTANCE *goes to it.* NICK *pours himself a glass of champagne.)*

CONSTANCE.   Yes? General Griggs isn't in, Rose. Oh. Yes. Just a minute. *(To* NICK) Rose Griggs wants to talk to *you.*

NICK.   What's the matter, she got some new trouble?

CONSTANCE *(Annoyed).*   Do you want the call or don't you?

NICK.   Tell her I'm busy.

CONSTANCE *(In phone).*   He's busy drinking, Rose. Shall I leave a message for General Griggs — Oh. *(She puts the phone down, annoyed)* She says it's absolutely and positively urgent that she speak with *you.* Not her husband. Absolutely and positively.

(She exits through hall. NICK *rises and goes to phone.)*

NICK.   Look here, my dear, don't be telling people you want to speak to me and not to your husband. Sounds awful. *(Laughs)* Oh. A most agreeable doctor. Must get to know him. Look, you don't have to convince me. Save it for your husband. Oh, come on. You're getting like those people who believe their own press agents. Anyway, I once knew a woman with heart trouble and it gave her a nice color. You didn't go to the doctor to believe him — *(Sighs, listens)* All right, of course I'm sorry. It sounds jolly nice and serious and I apologize. *(Listens)* Oh. Well, that is kind of you. Yes, tell your brother I'd like to stay with him. Oh, by Friday, certainly. How old is your niece? Is she the one with the braces on her teeth? (NINA *appears from the hall entrance. She is followed by* GRIGGS *who is carrying the picnic basket)* No, I won't paint anything out. That big a hack I'm not. Yes, we'll have plenty of time together. You're a good friend. *(To* NINA *and* GRIGGS*)* Had a nice day? *(Into phone)* No, I'm talking to your husband. Oh. Good-by. Take care of yourself. *(He hangs up. To* GRIGGS*)* That was Rose. *(Gaily, to* NINA*)* I've had a dull day, darling. (CROSSMAN *comes in)* Where'd you skip to?

NINA.   We drove over to Pass Christian.

NICK.   Did you put the car in the garage?

CROSSMAN *(Gives* NINA *the keys).*   Yes, all safe.

NICK.   Did you drive, Ned? That heavy Isotta? *(To* NINA*)* Nobody who drinks as much as Ned should be driving that car. Or any car belonging to me.

NINA.   And nobody as tight as you are should talk that way.

NICK *(Laughs).*   Have a drink, Ned.

> *(He brings* CROSSMAN *a glass.)*

CROSSMAN.   Thank you, no.

> (NICK *turns, hands glass to* GRIGGS.)

GRIGGS.   No, thank you.

NICK.   What the hell is this? Refusing to have a drink with me — *(To* CROSSMAN*)* I'm trying to apologize to you. Now take the drink —

NINA.　Nick, please —

NICK.　Stay out of it, Nina. Women don't know anything about the etiquette of drinking.

CROSSMAN *(Laughs)*.　Has it got etiquette now? *(As* NICK *again hands him glass. Shakes his head)* Thank you.

NICK *(Drunk, hurt)*.　Look here, old boy, I say in the light of what's happened, you've just got to take this. It's my way of apologizing and I shouldn't have to explain that to a gentleman.

(He grabs CROSSMAN'S *arm, playfully presses the glass to* CROSSMAN'S *lips.)*

CROSSMAN *(Quietly)*.　Don't do that.

NICK.　Come on, old boy. If I have to pour it down you —

CROSSMAN.　Don't do that.

*(*NICK, *laughing, presses the glass hard against* CROSSMAN'S *mouth.* CROSSMAN *pushes the glass and it falls to the floor.)*

NINA *(Sits down)*.　Well, we got rid of that glass. But there are plenty more, Nick.

NICK *(Sad, but firm to* CROSSMAN)*.*　Now *you've* put *yourself* on the defensive, my friend. That's always tactically unwise, isn't it, General Griggs?

GRIGGS.　I know nothing of tactics, Mr. Denery. Certainly not of yours.

NICK.　Then what the hell are you doing as a general?

GRIGGS.　Masquerading. They had a costume left over and they lent it to me.

NICK (*To* CROSSMAN). I'm waiting, Ned. Pour yourself a drink, and make *your* apologies.

CROSSMAN. You are just exactly the way I remember you. And that I wouldn't have believed of any man.

(He turns, goes out.)

NICK (*Like a hurt child*). What the hell does that mean? (*Calling*) Hey, Ned. Come on back and have it your way. (*Gets no answer, turns, hearty again*) Come on, General. Have a bottle with me.

NINA. Are we going to start again?

NICK. General, got something to tell you: your wife telephoned but she didn't want to speak to you.

GRIGGS. That's most understandable. Good night, Mrs. Denery, and thank you for a pleasant day.

NICK. But she'll want to speak to you in the morning. Better stick around in the morning.

GRIGGS (*Stares at him*). Thank you. Good night.

NICK (*Following him*). I think you're doing the wrong thing, wanting to leave Rose. You're going to be lonely at your age without —

GRIGGS. If my wife wishes to consult you, Mr. Denery, that's her business. But I don't wish to consult you.

(He exits.)

NICK. Sorry. Forget it.

(NICK *turns, takes his drink to the couch, lies down.*)

NINA (*After a pause*). You know, it's a nasty business hating yourself.

NICK. Who's silly enough to do that?

NINA. Me.

NICK *(Warmly)*. Come on over here, darling, and tell me about yourself. I've missed you.

NINA. To hate yourself, all the time.

NICK. I love you, Nina.

NINA *(Gets up)*. Here we go with that routine. Now you'll bait me until I tell you that you've never loved any woman, or any man, nor ever will. *(Wearily)* I'll be glad to get out of this house before Constance finds you out. She can go back to sleeping with her dreams. *(After a second)* You still think you can wind up everybody's affairs by Friday?

NICK. Oh, sure. Friday. Then we're going up to spend a month with Rose's brother, Henry something or other. In New Orleans.

NINA *(Carefully)*. What are you talking about?

NICK. Rose fixed it for me. I'm going to do a portrait of her niece, the heiress to the fortune. The girl is balding and has braces. *(Looks at her)* Five thousand dollars.

NINA. Are you crazy?

NICK. Not a bit.

NINA. It's all right to kid around here —

NICK *(Gets up)*. I *don't* know what you mean.

NINA *(Violently)*. Please don't let's talk this way. Just tell Mrs. Griggs that you've changed your mind —

NICK. I demand that you tell me what you mean.

NINA *(Angrily)*. How many years have we avoided saying it? Why must you walk into it now? *(Pauses, looks at him)* All right. Maybe it's time: you haven't finished a portrait in twelve years. And money isn't your reason for wanting to do this portrait. You're setting up a silly flirtation with Mrs. Griggs. I'm not going to New Orleans, Nick. I am not going to watch it all again. I can't go on this way with myself — *(Then softly)* Don't go. Call it off. You know how it will end. Please let's don't this time — We're not young any more, Nick. Somewhere we must have learned something.

NICK *(Softly, carefully)*. If I haven't finished every picture I started it's because I'm good enough to know they weren't good enough. All these years you never understood that? I think I will never forgive you for talking that way.

NINA. Your trouble is that you're an amateur, a gifted amateur. And like all amateurs you have very handsome reasons for what you do not finish — between trains and boats.

NICK. You have thought that about me, all these years?

NINA. Yes.

NICK. Then it was good of you and loyal to pretend you believed in me.

NINA. Good? Loyal? What do they mean? I loved you.

NICK. Yes, good and loyal. But I, too, have a little vanity — *(She laughs; he comes to her)* And no man can bear to live with a woman who feels that way about his work. I think you ought to leave tomorrow, Nina. For good and forever.

NINA *(Softly)*.   Yes. *(She turns)* Yes, of course. *(She starts to exit. He follows behind her, talking.)*

NICK.   But it must be different this time. Remember I said years ago — "Ten times of threatening is out, Nina," I said — the tenth time you stay gone.

NINA.   All right. Ten times is out. *(Quietly, desperately)* I promise for good and forever.

NICK *(She is climbing the staircase)*.   This time, spare yourself the return. And the begging and the self-humiliation and the self-hate. And the disgusting self-contempt. This time they won't do any good. *(He is following her but we cannot see him)* Let's write it down, darling. And have a drink to seal it.

(On the words "disgusting self-contempt," CONSTANCE *comes into the hall. She hears the words, recognizes* NICK'S *voice and stands, frowning, and thoughtful. Then she turns out the lights on the porch, puts on all lights except one lamp, comes back into the living room and begins to empty the ashtrays, etc.* SOPHIE *comes into the room carrying pillow, sheets, quilts, a glass of milk, and crosses to couch. Without speaking,* CONSTANCE *moves to help her and together they begin to make the couch for the night.)*

SOPHIE *(After a minute, smiles)*.   Do not worry for me, Aunt Constance.

CONSTANCE.   I can't help it.

SOPHIE. I think perhaps you worry sometimes in order that you should not think.

CONSTANCE (*Smiles*). Yes, maybe. I won't say any more. I'll be lonely without you, Sophie. I don't like being alone, any more. It's not a good way to live. And with you married, I'll be alone forever, unless — Well, Ned's loved me and it's been such a waste, such a waste. I know it now but — well — I don't know. (*Shyly, as a young girl would say it*) I wanted you to understand. You understand, Sophie? (SOPHIE *stares at her, frowning. Then* CONSTANCE *speaks happily*) Sleep well, dear.

(*She comes to* SOPHIE, *kisses her, exits, closing door.* SOPHIE *finishes with the bed, brings her milk to the bed table, takes off her robe, puts it around her shoulders, gets into bed, and lies quietly, thinking. Then she turns as she hears footsteps in the hall and she is staring at the door as* NICK *opens it. He trips over a chair, recovers himself, turns on a lamp.*)

NICK (*Sharply*). Constance! What is this — a boys' school with lights out at eleven! (*He sees* SOPHIE) Where's your aunt? I want to talk to her. What are you doing?

SOPHIE. I think I am asleep, Mr. Denery.

NICK. You're cute. Maybe too cute. (*He pours himself a drink*) I'm going down to the tavern and see if I can get up a beach party. Tell your aunt. Just tell her that. (*Going toward door*) Want to come? You couldn't be more welcome. (*She shakes her head*) Oh, come on. Throw on a coat. I'm not mad at you any more. *(He comes back toward her, looks down at her)* I couldn't paint you, Sophie. You're too thin. Damn shame you're so thin. *(Suddenly sits down on bed)* I'm sick of trouble. Aren't you? Like to drive away with me for a few days? *(Smiles at her)* Nobody would care. And we could be happy. I hate people not being happy. *(He lies down. His head is now on her knees)* Move your knees, baby, they're bony. And get me a drink.

SOPHIE.   Take the bottle upstairs, Mr. Denery.

NICK.   Get me a drink. And make it poison. *(Slowly, wearily, she gets up, takes his glass, goes to bottle, pours drink. He begins to sing. She brings glass back to him. He reaches up to take the glass, decides to pull her toward him, and spills the liquid on the bed)* Clumsy, honey, clumsy. But I'll forgive you.

(He is holding her, and laughing.)

SOPHIE *(Calmly)*.   Please go somewhere else, Mr. Denery.

NICK *(Springs up, drunk-angry)*.   People aren't usually rude to me, Sophie. Poor little girls always turn rude when they're about to marry rich little boys. What a life you're going to have. That boy doesn't even know what's the matter with him —

SOPHIE *(Very sharply)*.   Please, Mr. Denery, go away.

NICK *(Laughs)*.   Oh, you know what's the matter with him? No European would be as innocent of the world as you pretend. *(Delighted)* I tricked you into telling me. Know that?

SOPHIE.   You are drunk and I am tired. Please go away.

NICK *(Sits down across the room)*. Go to sleep, child. I'm not disturbing you. *(She stares at him, decides she can't move him, gets into bed, picks up a book, begins to read)* I won't say a word. Ssh. Sophie's reading. Do you like to read? Know the best way to read? With someone you love. Out loud. Ever try it that way, honey? *(He gets up, comes to bed, stands near her, speaking over her shoulder)* I used to know a lot of poetry. Brought up on Millay. My candle and all that. "I had to be a liar. My mother was a leprechaun, my father was a friar." Crazy for the girl. *(Leans over and kisses her hair) (She pulls her head away)* Ever wash your hair in champagne, darling? I knew a woman once. *(Tips the glass over her head)* Let's try it.

SOPHIE *(Sharply)*. Let us not try it again.

NICK *(Sits down beside her)*. Now for God's sake don't get angry. *(Takes her shoulders and shakes her)* I'm sick of angry women. All men are sick of angry women, if angry women knew the truth. Sophie, we can always go away and starve. I'll manage to fall in love with you.

SOPHIE *(He is holding her)*. Mr. Denery, I am sick of you.

NICK *(Softly)*. Tell me you don't like me and I will go away and not come back.

SOPHIE.   No, sir. I do not like you.

NICK.   People have hated me. But nobody's ever not liked me. If I thought you weren't flirting, I'd be hurt. Is there any aspirin downstairs? If you kiss me, Sophie, be kind to me for just a minute, I'll go away. I may come back another day, but I'll go all by myself — *(Desperately)* Please, Sophie, please.

SOPHIE *(Sighs, holds up her side face to him).*   All right. Then you will go, remember. *(He takes her in his arms, pulls her down on the bed. She struggles to get away from him. She speaks angrily)* Do not make yourself such a clown. *(When she cannot get away from him)* I will call your wife, Mr. Denery.

NICK *(Delighted).*   That would be fun, go ahead. We're getting a divorce. Sophie, let's make this night our night. God, Julie, if you only knew what I've been through —

SOPHIE *(Violently).*   Oh shut up.

(She pulls away from him with great effort. He catches her robe and rolls over on it.)

NICK *(Giggles as he settles down comfortably).* Come on back. It's nice and warm here and I love you very much. But we've got to get some sleep, darling. Really we have to.

(Then he turns over and lies still. She stands looking at him.)

SOPHIE *(After a minute).*   Get up, Mr. Denery. I will help you upstairs. *(No answer)* Please, please get up.

NICK *(Gently, half passed-out).*   It's raining out. Just tell the concierge I'm your brother. She'll understa — *(The words fade off.* SOPHIE *waits a second and then leans over and with great strength begins to shake him)* Stop that. *(He passes out, begins to breathe heavily. She turns, goes to hall, stands at the foot of the steps. Then she changes her mind and comes back into the room. She goes to the couch, stands, looking at him, decides to pull him by the legs) (Softly)* I'll go away in a few minutes. Don't be so young. Have a little pity. I am old and sick.

> (SOPHIE *draws back, moves slowly to the other side of the room as the curtain falls.)*

CURTAIN

ACT THREE

SCENE:

> Seven o'clock *the next morning.* Nick *is asleep on the couch.* Sophie *is sitting in a chair, drinking a cup of coffee. A minute after the rise of the curtain,* Mrs. Ellis *comes down the steps, comes into the room.*

Mrs. Ellis. I heard you bumping around in the kitchen, Sophie. The older you get the less you sleep, and the more you look forward to meals. Particularly breakfast, because you've been alone all night, and the nights are the hardest — *(She sees* Nick, *stares, moves over to look at him.)* What is this?

Sophie. It is Mr. Denery.

Mrs. Ellis *(Turns to stare at her).* What's he doing down here?

Sophie. He became drunk and went to sleep.

Mrs. Ellis. He has been here all night? *(*Sophie *nods)* What's the matter with you? Get him out of here immediately.

Sophie. I cannot move him. I tried. Shall I get you some coffee?

Mrs. Ellis *(Staring at her).* Are you being silly, Sophie? Sometimes it is very hard to tell with you. Why didn't you call Constance or Mrs. Denery?

SOPHIE.   I did not know what to do. Mr. and Mrs.
Denery had some trouble between them, or so he said,
and I thought it might be worse for her if — (Smiles)
Is it so much? He was just a little foolish and sleepy.
(Goes toward door) I will get Leon and Sadie and we
will take him upstairs.

MRS. ELLIS (Crosses to door). You will not get
Leon and Sadie. Rose Griggs may be President of the
gossip club for summer Anglo-Saxons, but Leon is certainly President of the Negro chapter. You will get this,
er, out of here before anybody else sees him. (She
crosses back to bed, pulls blanket off NICK) At least he's
dressed. Bring me that cup of coffee. (SOPHIE brings
cup) Mr. Denery! Sit up! (NICK moves his head
slightly. To SOPHIE) Hold his head up.

(SOPHIE holds NICK's head; MRS. ELLIS tries to
make him drink.)

NICK (Very softly).   Please leave me alone.

MRS. ELLIS (Shouting in his ear).   Mr. Denery, listen to me. You are to get up and get out of here immediately.

NICK (Giving a bewildered look around the room;
then he closes his eyes).   Julie.

SOPHIE.   He has been speaking of Julie most of the
night.

MRS. ELLIS (Very sharply).   Shall I wake your wife
and see if she can locate Julie for you, or would you
rather be cremated here? Get up, Mr. Denery. (He
opens his eyes, shuts them again.)

SOPHIE.   You see how it is? (She tries to pull her

robe from under him.) Would you get off my robe, Mr. Denery?

MRS. ELLIS *(Stares at her)*. Sophie, you're a damned little ninny. *(Very loudly, to* NICK*)* Now get up. You have no right to be here. You must get up immediately. I say *you,* you get up. *(Shouting)* Get to your room. Get out of here.

NICK *(Turns, opens his eyes, half sits up, speaks gently)*. Don't scream at me, Mrs. Ellis. *(Sees* SOPHIE*, begins to realize where he is, groans deeply)* I passed out?

SOPHIE. Yes, sir. Most deeply.

MRS. ELLIS. I'm sure after this he won't mind if you don't call him "sir."

NICK. Champagne's always been a lousy drink for me. How did I get down here? *(He turns over)* I'm sorry, child. What happened?

SOPHIE. You fell asleep.

NICK *(Hesitantly)*. Did I — God, I'm a fool. What did I — Did I do anything or say anything? Tell me, Sophie.

MRS. ELLIS. Please get up and get out of here.

NICK. I'm thirsty. I want a quart of water. Or a bottle of beer. Get me a bottle of cold beer, Sophie, will you? *(Looks around the bed)* Where'd you sleep? Get me the beer, will you?

MRS. ELLIS *(Carefully)*. Mr. Denery, you are in Sophie's bed, in the living room of a house in a small Southern town where for a hundred and fifty years it has been impossible to take a daily bath without everybody in town advising you not to dry out your skin. You know that as well as I do. Now get up and go out by the side lawn to the boathouse. Put your head under water, or however you usually treat these matters, and come back through the front door for breakfast.

NICK *(Laughs).* I couldn't eat breakfast.

MRS. ELLIS. I don't find you cute. I find only that you can harm a young girl. Do please understand that.

NICK. Yes, I do. And I'm sorry. *(He sits up, untangling himself from the robe)* What's this? Oh, Sophie, child, I must have been a nuisance. I am *so* sorry.

MRS. ELLIS *(Very loudly).* Get up and get the hell out of here.

(The door opens and ROSE, *carrying her overnight handbag, sticks her head in.)*

ROSE *(To* MRS. ELLIS, *who is directly on a line with the door).* You frightened me. I could hear you outside on the lawn, so early. Oh, Nick. How nice you're downstairs. I never expected it — *(Her voice trails off as she sees* SOPHIE *and realizes* NICK *is on the bed)* Oh. *(Giggles, hesitantly)* You look like you just woke up, Nick. I mean, just woke up where you are.

MRS. ELLIS *(To* NICK). Well, that's that. Perhaps you wanted it this way, Mr. Denery.

(She starts out as LEON *appears carrying the coffee urn.* ROSE *stands staring at* NICK.)*

LEON *(Very curious, but very hesitant in doorway).* Should I put it here this morning, like every day, or —

MRS. ELLIS. Who told you, Leon?

LEON.   Told me what, Mrs. Ellis? Sadie says take on in the urn —

MRS. ELLIS.   I'm not talking about the urn. Who told you about Mr. Denery being here?

LEON.   Told me? Why Miss Sophie came in for coffee for them.

MRS. ELLIS *(After a second, shrugs, points to coffee urn).*   Take it into the dining room.

LEON.   You want me come back and straighten up, Miss Sophie?

MRS. ELLIS *(Waves him out).*   Mrs. Griggs will be glad to straighten up.

(She exits.)

ROSE *(Softly to* NICK*).*   You were here all night? I come back needing your help and advice as I've never before needed anything. And I find you —

NICK.   Rose, please stop moving about. You're making me seasick. And would you go outside? I'd like to speak to Sophie.

ROSE.   I am waiting for you to explain, Nick. I don't understand.

NICK.   There is no need for you to understand.

ROSE.   I'm not judging you. I know that there's probably a good explanation — But please tell me, Nick, what happened and then I won't be angry.

NICK.   What the hell are you talking about? What's it your business? Now go upstairs, Rose.

ROSE *(Softly, indignant).*   "Go upstairs, Rose." "What's it your business?" After I work my head off getting the commission of the portrait for you and after

I go to the doctor's on your advice, although I never would have gone if I had known, and I come back here and find you this way. *(Sits down.)* You've hurt me and you picked a mighty bad day to do it.

> *(The door opens and* CONSTANCE *comes in. She goes to* NICK, *stands looking at him.)*

CONSTANCE.   Nick, I want you to go to that window and look across the street. *(He stares at her. Then he gets up slowly and slowly moves to the window)* The Carters have three extra guests on their breakfast porch, the Gable sisters are unexpectedly entertaining — *(With feeling)* This house was not built to be stared at.

NICK *(Gently).*   It can't be that bad, Constance.

CONSTANCE.   It is just that bad.

NICK.   I'm sorry. I was silly and drunk but there's no sense making more out of it than that.

CONSTANCE.   I am not making anything out of it. But I know what is being made out of it. In your elegant way of life, I daresay this is an ordinary occurrence. But not in our village. *(The telephone rings.* CONSTANCE *picks up phone, says "Hello," pauses, "Hello, Mrs. Sims." Then her face becomes angry and she hangs up. She stands looking at the phone, and then takes it off the hook. Turns to* NICK) Please explain to me what happened. *(Points to telephone and then across the street)* I only know what they know.

SOPHIE.   Mr. Denery came down looking for someone to talk to. He saw me, recited a little poetry, spoke to me of his troubles, tried to embrace me in a most mild fashion. He was uncertain of my name and continued throughout the night to call me Julie although twice he called for Cecile. And fell into so deep a sleep that I could not move him. Alcohol. It is the same in my country, every country.

CONSTANCE (*Softly, as if it pained her*). You are taking a very light tone about it, Sophie.

SOPHIE (*Turns away, goes toward couch, and through the next speeches will strip the bed and pile the clothes*). I will speak whichever way you think most fits the drama, Aunt Constance.

CONSTANCE. Will you tell me why you stayed in the room? Why didn't you come and call me, or —

NICK. Oh, look here. It's obvious. The kid didn't want to make any fuss and thought I'd wake up and go any minute. Damn nice of you, Sophie, and I'm grateful.

CONSTANCE. It was the most dangerous "niceness" I've ever heard of.

(SOPHIE *looks up, stares at* CONSTANCE.)

NICK. I know it's hard for you, Constance, but it's not all that much.

CONSTANCE. Isn't it? You've looked out of the window. Now go down to the drugstore and listen to them and I think you'll change your mind.

NICK. Look. A foolish guy drinks, passes out —

ROSE (*Amazed as she turns to look at* SOPHIE). Why look at Sophie. Just as calm as can be. Making the bed. Like it happened to her every night.

CONSTANCE (*Turns, realizes* ROSE *is in the room*). What are you doing here, Rose?

Rose. Sitting here thinking that no man sleeps in girl's bed unless she gives him to understand — (constance *stares at her*) You can blame Nick all you like. But you know very well that a nice girl would have screamed.

Constance. How dare you talk this way? Whatever gave you the right — I hope it will be convenient for you to leave today. I will apologize to the General.

Rose *(Softly)*. That's all right, Constance. I must leave today, in any case. You see, I have to — *(Sighs, sincerely)* You won't be mad at me for long when you know the story. Oh, I'm very tired now. Could I have my breakfast in bed? Doctor's orders. *(She goes out, passes* crossman *who is coming in. In sepulchral tones)* Good morning, dear Ned. *(Then in a sudden burst)* Have you heard — ?

Crossman *(Cheerful)*. Good morning. Yes, I've heard. I'm not the one deaf man in town.

(Passes her. She stares at his back, reluctantly exits.)

Constance *(Turns)*. Ned, what should we do?

Crossman. Is there always something that can be done, remedied, patched, pulled apart and put together again? There is nothing to "do," Con. *(Smiles to* sophie, *amused)* How are you, Sophie?

Sophie. I am all right, Mr. Ned.

Nick. Ned, is it as bad as *(Gestures toward window and* constance) Constance thinks?

Constance. What's the difference to you? You're

just sitting there telling yourself what provincial people we are and how you wish you were in the Ritz bar with people who would find it amusing with their lunch. *(Very angrily)* You came here as my friend and in our small life — in our terms — you have dishonored my house. It has taken me too many years to find out that you —

CROSSMAN.   All right, Con, maybe that's the truth; but what's the good of discussing Nick's character and habits now?

NICK *(Sincerely, to* CONSTANCE*)*.   Whatever you think of me, I didn't want this. I know what it will mean to Sophie and I'll stay here and face anything that will help you. Anything I can say or do —

SOPHIE *(She finishes folding the clothes)*.   What will it "mean" to me, Mr. Ned?

CONSTANCE *(Softly)*.   You're old enough to know. And I believe you do know.

SOPHIE.   I want to know from Mr. Ned what he thinks.

CROSSMAN *(To* SOPHIE*)*.   I know what you want to know: the Ellis name is a powerful name. They won't be gossiped about out loud. They won't gossip about you and they won't listen to gossip about you. In their own way they'll take care of things. *(Carefully)* You can be quite sure of that. Quite sure.

SOPHIE *(After a second)*.   And that is all?

CROSSMAN.   That is all.

SOPHIE *(Softly, carefully)*.   Thank you, Mr. Ned.

CONSTANCE.   Take care of things? She hasn't done

anything. Except be stupid. The Tuckerman name is as good as the Ellis name —

CROSSMAN. Yes, yes. Sure enough.

(SOPHIE *looks at* CROSSMAN, *exits. She passes* LEON *in the hall. He is carrying his hat.*)

LEON. Mrs. Ellis is cutting up about her breakfast. And Sadie's waiting for orders. We're messed this morning, for good.

CONSTANCE. Not at all. Tell Sadie I'm coming. *(She goes toward door)* What's your hat for, Leon?

LEON. Well, kind of a hot sun today.

CONSTANCE. Not in here. Rest your hat: you'll have plenty of time to gossip when the sun goes down.

(She goes out.)

NICK *(Miserably)*. Ned. Ned, you understand I never thought it would make all this — Is Constance being — I mean, is she being old-maid fussy or is it really unpleasant —

CROSSMAN. It is unpleasant. She loves the girl, and she's worried for her.

NICK *(Groans)*. If I could do something —

CROSSMAN. You did; but don't make too much of it.

NICK *(The first kind word he's heard)*. Thank you, boy.

CROSSMAN. Or too little. (NICK *groans*) Nobody will blame you too much. The girl's a foreigner and they don't understand her and therefore don't like her. You're a home-town boy and as such you didn't do anything they wouldn't do. Boys will be boys and in the South there's no age limit on boyishness. Therefore, she led you on, or whatever is this morning's phrase. You'll come off all right. But then I imagine you always do.

NICK.   You think this is coming off all right?

CROSSMAN.   No, I don't.

NICK.   I didn't even want her. Never thought of her that way.

CROSSMAN (*Too sympathetic*).   That *is* too bad. Better luck next time. You're young — in spirit.

(*He exits into hall toward dining room as* HILDA, *carrying a jewel case, and hat box, comes down the steps. She has on her hat and gloves.*)

NICK (*Who is sitting on a line with the door and sees her, speaks in German*).   Where you going?

HILDA (*In German*).   Good morning, sir. I am taking madame's luggage to the nine-thirty train.

(*She moves off as* NINA *appears.* NINA *has on a hat and gloves. On her heels is* ROSE *in a fluffy negligee.* ROSE *is talking as she follows* NINA *down the steps.*)

ROSE.   I'm not trying to excuse him. Of course it was indiscreet but you're a woman of the world, Nina, and you know what young girls are with a tipsy man. Nina, do believe that I saw them this morning and he didn't have the slightest interest in her. Nina —

NINA (*Turns to her, very pleasantly*).   I know it's eccentric of me, Mrs. Griggs, but I dislike being called by my first name before midnight.

Rose *(Hurt, softly).*   You shouldn't allow yourself such a nasty snub. I'm only trying to help Nick. I know him well enough to know that he didn't do a thing — (NINA *laughs*) He's been my good friend. I'm trying to be a friend to him.

Nina.   You will have every opportunity.

Nick *(Very angry).*   Will you please not stand there in the hall discussing me?

Rose.   Oh! *(Looks at* NICK, *then at* NINA, *steps back into hall, calls toward kitchen)* Leon! Could I have my tray upstairs? *(As she goes past room and upstairs)* Anybody seen my husband this morning?
                    (Exits.)

Nick.   Nina. *(She comes in)* I just want to say before you go that they're making an awful row about nothing —

Nina.   You don't owe me an explanation, Nick.

Nick.   Nothing happened, Nina, I swear. Nothing happened.

Nina.   Try out phrases like "nothing happened" on women like Mrs. Griggs.

Nick *(Smiles).*   I'm sorry as all hell but they sure are cutting up —

Nina.   Well, it is a tasty little story. Particularly for a girl who is going to be married.

Nick.   My God, I'd forgotten about the boy. I must say he's an easy boy to forget about. Now I'll have to take *him* out and explain —

Nina.   Don't do that, Nick. He isn't a fool.

Nick *(Looks around, thinking of anything to keep*

her in the room).   Shall I get you a cup of coffee, darling?

NINA.   No. Darling will have it on the train.
(She turns.)

NICK.   Nina, I swear I didn't sleep with her.

NINA.   I believe you. The girl doesn't like you.

NICK.   Doesn't she? She's been very kind to me. She could have raised hell. That doesn't sound as if she doesn't like me. (NINA *laughs*) Don't laugh at me this morning. *(After a second)* What can I do for her, Nina?

NINA.   You used to send wicker hampers of white roses. With a card saying "White for purity and sad parting."

NICK.   Stop being nasty to me. *(Then he smiles and comes toward her)* Or maybe it's a good sign.

NINA.   It isn't. I just say these things by rote. *(Turns)* I don't know how long I'll be in New York, but you can call Horace and he'll take care of the legal stuff for us.

NICK *(Close to her).*   I told you last night that I would agree to the separation because I knew with what justice you wanted to leave me.

NINA *(Coldly).*   That's not at all what you said.

NICK.   I was tight. It was what I meant to say —

NINA *(Very angry).*   You're lying. You said just what you meant to say: I was to leave. And not make you sick with my usual begging to come back —

NICK.   Stop, Nina. Take any kind of revenge you want, but — please — some other day. *(Leans down, puts his face against her face)* Don't leave me. Don't ever leave me. We've had good times, wild times. They made up for what was bad and they always will. Most people don't get that much. We've only had one trouble; you hate yourself for loving me. Because you have contempt for me.

NINA. For myself. I have no right —

NICK. No, nobody has. No right at all.

NINA. I wouldn't have married you, Nick, if I had known —

NICK. You would have married me. Or somebody like me. You've needed to look down on me, darling. You've needed to make fun of me. And to be ashamed of yourself for doing it.

NINA *(Softly)*. Am I that sick?

NICK. I don't know about such words. You found the man you deserved. That's all. I am no better and no worse than what you really wanted. You like to — to demean yourself. And so you chose me. You must say I haven't minded much. Because I've always loved you and known we'd last it out. Come back to me, Nina, without shame in wanting to. *(He leans down, kisses her neck)* Put up with me a little longer, kid. I'm getting older and I'll soon wear down.

NINA *(She smiles, touched)*. I've never heard you speak of getting old.

NICK *(Quickly)*. Yes. *(Then)* The *Ile* sails next week. Let's get on. We'll have fun. Tell me we're together again and you're happy. Say it, Nina, quick.

NINA. I'm happy.

(He takes her in his arms, kisses her. Then he stands away, looks at her, and smiles shyly.)

NICK.   There'll be no more of what you call my "home-comings." Old friends and all that. They are damn bores, with empty lives.

NINA.   Is that so different from us?

NICK.   If we could only do something for the kid. Take her with us, get her out of here until they get tired of the gossip —

NINA *(Laughs).*   I don't think we will take her with us.

NICK *(Laughs).*   Now, now. You know what I mean.

NINA.   I know what you mean — and we're not taking her with us.

NICK.   I suppose there isn't anything to do. *(Softly, his hand to his head)* I feel sick, Nina.

NINA.   You've got a hangover.

NICK.   It's more than that. I've got a sore throat and my back aches. Come on, darling, let's get on the train.

NINA.   You go. I'll stay and see if there's anything I can do. That's what you really want. Go on, Nicky. Maybe it's best.

NICK.   I couldn't do that.

NINA.   Don't waste time, darling. You'll miss the train. I'll bring your clothes with me.

NICK *(Laughs, ruefully).*   If you didn't see through me so fast, you wouldn't dislike yourself so much.

(Comes to her) You're a wonderful girl. It's wonderful of you to take all this on —

NINA.   I've had practice. —

NICK *(Hurt)*. That's not true. You know this never happened before.

NINA *(Smiles)*.   Nicky, it always confuses you that the fifth time something happens it varies slightly from the second and fourth. No, it never happened in this house before. Cora had a husband and Sylvia wanted one. And this isn't a hotel in Antibes, and Sophie is not a rich Egyptian. And this time you didn't break your arm on a boat deck and it isn't 1928 —

NICK. This is your day, Nina. But pass up the chance to play it too hard, will you? Take me or leave me now but don't —

NINA. You're right. Please go, darling. Your staying won't do any good. Neither will mine, but maybe —

NICK.   When will you come? I tell you what: you take the car and drive to Mobile. I'll get off there and wait at the Battle House. Then we can drive the rest of the way together. Must be somewhere in Mobile I can waste time for a few hours —

NINA *(Gaily)*. I'm sure. But let's have a week's rest. Now go on.

NICK *(Takes her in his arms)*. I love you, Nina. And we'll have the best time of our lives. Good luck, darling. And thank you. *(He kisses her)* They won't rag you, nobody ever does. We'll get the bridal suite on the *Ile* and have all our meals in bed. *(He moves away)* If you possibly can, bring the new portrait with you. I can finish it now. And try to get me the old portrait, darling. Maybe Constance will sell it to you — (NINA *laughs*) All right. Think what you want and I'll be what I am. I love you and you love me and that's that and always will be.

(He exits. She stands quietly.)

NINA.   You love me and I love you and that's that and always will be. *(Then she turns, goes to the bell cord, pulls it. After a second,* CONSTANCE *appears in the hall.* NINA *does not turn)* Leon, could I have breakfast on the porch?

CONSTANCE *(In the doorway. She is carrying a tray).* Yes, of course. I'll tell Leon to bring it.

*(*NINA *turns, stares at her.)*

NINA.   I am very sorry, Constance.

CONSTANCE.   I am sorry, too, my dear.

NINA.   I don't know what else to say. I wish —

CONSTANCE.   There's nothing for us to say. *(There is an awkward pause)* Well. I'll tell Leon. Old lady Ellis is having her second breakfast. She always does on her last day. I don't know why. *(She starts out as* CARRIE, *followed by* FREDERICK, *comes down the steps.* CARRIE *has on her hat, etc., as if she were ready for traveling.* FREDERICK *is carrying two valises)* Shall I send breakfast up to Nick?

NINA *(Very quickly).*   No, no. I'll just have mine and —

FREDERICK (*Calling to* CONSTANCE). Where's Sophie?

CONSTANCE. I'll send her in.

FREDERICK (*Smiles*). Don't sound so solemn, Miss Constance.

CONSTANCE (*Sharply*). I didn't mean to.

(*She disappears in the direction of the dining room.* FREDERICK *and* CARRIE *come into the room.*)

NINA. Mr. Ellis, I should be carrying a sign that says my husband is deeply sorry and so am I.

(*He smiles at her. She turns, goes out on the porch, closes the door behind her.*)

CARRIE (*Hesitantly*). She's a nice woman, I think. Must be a hard life for her.

FREDERICK (*Laughs*). I don't think so. (*Turns as he hears* SOPHIE *in the hall*) Now remember, Mother. (SOPHIE *appears in the door.* FREDERICK *goes to her, takes her chin in his hand, kisses her*) I want to tell you something fast. I don't know how to explain it but I'm kind of glad this foolishness happened. It makes you seem closer to me, some silly way. You must believe that, although I can't make it clear. Now there are two things to do right away. Your choice.

SOPHIE. I have made bad gossip for you, Frederick. We must speak about that. Right away.

FREDERICK. There's no need to speak about it again. It's a comic story and that's all. And you must begin to laugh about it.

SOPHIE *(Smiles)*. I did laugh but nobody would laugh with me. And nobody will laugh in New Orleans, either. Is that not so, Mrs. Ellis?

CARRIE. I think you should travel up with us, Sophie. Right now. Whatever is to be faced, we will do much better if we face it all together and do it quickly.

FREDERICK *(Looks at her, as if they had had previous talk)*. You're putting it much too importantly. There's nothing to be faced.

CARRIE. I didn't mean to make it too important. Of course, it isn't —

SOPHIE *(Puts her hand on his arm)*. It is important to you. And you must not be kind and pretend that —

FREDERICK *(Firmly)*. I'm not being kind. I told you the truth. I've been in trouble, now you've been in a little. That's all, now or ever. *(Shyly)* As far as I'm concerned, it makes us seem less like strangers. I'd hope you'd feel the same way —

CARRIE *(Quickly)*. Run and pack a bag, Sophie. It's a lovely day for driving and we'll be in town for lunch. I think you and I will have it at the club — Now let's not talk about it any more —

SOPHIE. No. It would be most mistaken of me to come now. My leaving here would seem as if I must be ashamed and you shamed for me. I must not come with you today. I must stay here. *(Smiles)* It must be faced.

FREDERICK. All right. That makes sense. Mother and Grandma will drive up and I'll stay here —

SOPHIE *(Very quickly)*. No, no. You must not stay

here. *(Points to window, meaning town)* They knew you had made plans to leave today as usual. And so you must leave. We must act as if nothing had happened, and if we do that, and are not worried, it will all end more quickly. *(Goes to* FREDERICK*)* Believe me, Frederick. You know what I say is true. All must seem to be as it has been. *(To* MRS. ELLIS*)* You tell him that, please, Mrs. Ellis.

CARRIE.   I don't know. You belong with us now, Sophie. We don't want to leave you, or Constance. I think she should come along and —

SOPHIE.   Oh, she would not do that. You know she would not. *(Smiles, very cheerful)* Now. You are both very kind. But you know what I say is best for us all, and of no importance whether I come one week or the next. *(Takes* FREDERICK'S *arm)* You have said I must laugh about it. I do laugh, and so it will be nothing for me to stay.

(MRS. ELLIS *comes to the door from the direction of the dining room.)*

CARRIE.   Good-by, Sophie. We will be waiting for you.

(She exits, passing MRS. ELLIS *without speaking.)*

FREDERICK *(Unhappily)*.   You all seem to know what's right, what's best, so much faster than I do. I —

SOPHIE *(Smiles, puts her hand over his mouth)*. This is best. Please.

FREDERICK.   Then let us come back this week end. Can I do that?

SOPHIE *(She touches his face).* I think so. You are a nice man, Frederick.

FREDERICK *(Kisses her).* And you're a nice girl to think so. See you in a few days. *(Turns to go out, passes* MRS. ELLIS*)* I feel happy, Grandma.

(MRS. ELLIS *nods, waits for him to exit.* SOPHIE *sits down.)*

MRS. ELLIS *(After a second).* Sophie.

SOPHIE *(Smiles as if she knew what was coming).* Yes.

MRS. ELLIS. Did *Carrie* ask you to leave with us? (SOPHIE *nods)* Ah. That's not good. When Carrie gets smart she gets very smart. Sophie, Frederick meant what he said to you. But I know them both and I would guess that in a week, or two or three, he will agree to go to Europe with his mother and he will tell you that it is only a postponement. And he will believe what he says. Time and decisions melt and merge for him and ten years from now he will be convinced that you refused to marry him. And he will always be a little sad about what could have been.

SOPHIE. Yes. Of course.

MRS. ELLIS. Carrie never will want him to marry. And she will never know it. Well, she, too, got cheated a long time ago. There is very little I can do — perhaps very little I want to do any more. Don't judge him too harshly, child.

SOPHIE *(Smiles).* No, I will not judge. I will write a letter to him.

MRS. ELLIS. That's my girl. Don't take from us

what you don't have to take, or waste yourself on defeat. *(She gets up)* Oh, Sophie, feel sorry for Frederick. He is nice and he is nothing. And his father before him and my other sons. And myself. Another way. Well. If there is ever a chance, come and see me.

> *(She moves out.* SOPHIE *remains seated. After a second* CONSTANCE *comes in from the hall. She looks at* SOPHIE.)

CONSTANCE *(Hesitantly)*.   Carrie tells me you'll be going up to town in a few weeks to stay with them. I'm glad. *(No answer)* Er. Why don't you go up to my room, dear, and lie down for a while? *(Points to porch)* She's on the porch. I'm going to ask the Denerys to leave today. I am sure they will want to, anyway. And the Griggses will be going and then just you and I —

SOPHIE.   I will not be going to New Orleans, Aunt Constance, and there will be no marriage between Frederick and me.

CONSTANCE *(Stares at her)*.   But Carrie told me —

SOPHIE.   Now she believes that she wants me. But it will not be so.

CONSTANCE *(After a second)*.   I wish I could say I was surprised or angry. But I'm not sorry. No marriage without love —

SOPHIE *(Pleasantly)*.   Yes. Yes.

CONSTANCE *(Gently)*.   You're not to feel bad or hurt.

SOPHIE.   I do not.

CONSTANCE.   I'm — I'm glad. Mighty glad. Everything will work out for the best. You'll see. After everybody goes, we'll get the house and the accounts cleaned up and straightened out as usual. *(Gaily)* And then I think you and I will take a little trip. I haven't seen Memphis in years and maybe in a few months — *(Gently)* You know what? We can even sell, rent, the place, if we want to. We can pick up and go anywhere we want. You'll see, dear. We'll have a nice time.

SOPHIE *(Almost as if she were speaking to a child).* Yes, Aunt Constance.

> (CONSTANCE *goes out.* SOPHIE *turns to watch* LEON *who, during* CONSTANCE'S *speech, has come out on the porch and is serving breakfast to* NINA. SOPHIE *rises and goes out to the porch. She takes the coffee pot from* LEON — *he has finished placing the other dishes* — *nods to him, and pours* NINA'S *coffee.* LEON *exits.* NINA *turns, sees* SOPHIE, *turns back.)*

You are a pretty woman, Mrs. Denery, when your face is happy.

NINA.   And you think my face is happy *this* morning?

SOPHIE.   Oh, yes. You and Mr. Denery have had a nice reconciliation.

NINA *(Stares at her).*   Er. Yes, I suppose so.

SOPHIE.   I am glad for you. That is as it has been and will always be. *(She sits down)* Now could I speak with you and Mr. Denery?

NINA *(Uncomfortably).*   Sophie, if there was anything I can do — Er. Nick isn't here. I thought it best for us all —

SOPHIE *(Softly).*   Ah. Ah, my aunt will be most sad.

NINA.   Sophie, there's no good my telling you how sorry, how — What can I do?

SOPHIE.   You can give me five thousand dollars, Mrs. Denery. American dollars, of course. *(Demurely; her accent from now on grows more pronounced)* I have been subjected to the most degrading experience from which no young girl easily recovers. *(In French)* A most degrading experience from which no young girl easily recovers —

NINA *(Stares at her).*   It sounds exactly the same in French.

SOPHIE.   Somehow sex and money are simpler in French. Well. In English, then, I have lost or will lose my most beloved fiancé; I cannot return to school and the comrades with whom my life has been so happy; my aunt is uncomfortable and unhappy in the only life she knows and is now burdened with me for many years to come. I am utterly, utterly miserable, Mrs. Denery. I am ruined. (NINA *bursts out laughing.* SOPHIE *smiles)* Please do not laugh at me.

NINA.   I suppose I should be grateful to you for making a joke of it.

SOPHIE.   You make a mistake. I am most serious.

NINA *(Stops laughing).*   Are you? Sophie, it is an unpleasant and foolish incident and I don't wish to minimize it. But don't you feel you're adding considerable drama to it?

SOPHIE.   No, ma'am. I did not say that is the way

I thought of it. But that is the way it will be considered in this place, in this life. Little is made into very much here.

NINA.   It's just the same in your country.

SOPHIE.   No, Mrs. Denery. You mean it is the same in Brussels or Strasbourg or Paris, with those whom you would meet. In my class, in my town, it is not so. In a poor house if a man falls asleep drunk — and certainly it happens with us each Saturday night — he is not alone with an innocent young girl because the young girl, at my age, is not so innocent and because her family is in the same room, not having any other place to go. It arranges itself differently; you have more rooms and therefore more troubles.

NINA.   Yes. I understand the lecture. (*Pauses*) Why do you want five thousand dollars, Sophie?

SOPHIE.   I wish to go home.

NINA *(Gently)*.   Then I will be happy to give it to you. Happier than you know to think we can do something.

SOPHIE.   Yes. I am sure. But I will not accept it as largesse — to make you happy. We will call it a loan, come by through blackmail. One does not have to be grateful for blackmail money, nor think of oneself as a charity girl.

NINA *(After a second)*.   Blackmail money?

SOPHIE.   Yes ma'am. You will give me five thousand dollars because if you do not I will say that Mr. Denery seduced me last night. (NINA *stares at her, laughs*) You are gay this morning, madame.

NINA *(Shocked).* Sophie, Sophie. What a child you are. It's not necessary to talk this way.

SOPHIE. I wish to prevent you from giving favors to me.

NINA. I intended no favors. And I don't like this kind of talk. Nick did not seduce you and I want no more jokes about it. *(Pleasantly)* Suppose we try to be friends —

SOPHIE. I am not joking, Mrs. Denery. And I do not wish us to be friends.

NINA *(Gets up).* I would like to give you the money. And I will give it to you for that reason and no other.

SOPHIE. It does not matter to me what you would like. You will give it to me for my reason — or I will not take it.

(Angrily, NINA *goes toward door, goes into the room, then turns and smiles at* SOPHIE.*)*

NINA. You are serious? Just for a word, a way of calling something, you would hurt my husband and me?

SOPHIE. For me it is more than a way of calling something.

NINA. You're a tough little girl.

SOPHIE. Don't you think people often say other people are tough when they do not know how to cheat them?

NINA *(Angrily).* I was not trying to cheat you of anything —

SOPHIE. Yes, you were. You wish to be the kind

lady who most honorably stays to discharge — within reason — her obligations. And who goes off, as she has gone off many other times, to make the reconciliation with her husband. How would you and Mr. Denery go on living without such incidents as me? I have been able to give you a second, or a twentieth, honeymoon.

NINA *(Angrily)*.   Is that speech made before you raise your price?

SOPHIE *(Smiles)*.   No. A blackmail bargain is still a bargain.

(CROSSMAN *appears in the hall,* SOPHIE *sees him.)*

NINA.   How would — How shall we make the arrangements?

SOPHIE *(Calling)*.   Mr. Ned. *(Pleasantly, to* NINA*)* Mr. Ned will know what to do.

NINA *(After a second to* CROSSMAN*)*.   I'd like to get a check cashed. It's rather a large check. Could you vouch for me at the bank?

CROSSMAN.   Sure. That's easy enough. The bank's just around the corner.

SOPHIE.   Would you like me to come with you, Mrs. Denery?

NINA *(Smiles)*.   You know, I think perhaps it's wisest for you to stay right here. You and I in a bank, cashing a check, this morning, could well be interpreted as a pay-off, or blackmail.

(She goes out.)

SOPHIE.   I will be going home, Mr. Ned.

CROSSMAN *(Smiles)*.   Good. *(Looks at her, turns to*

stare at NINA, *as she passes him and goes into hall)* At least I hope it's good.

SOPHIE.   I think it is more good than it is not good.
(He goes out.)

(ROSE *comes down the steps. Her manner is hurried, nervous. She goes immediately to windows. She looks out as if she saw somebody coming. Then she turns and sees* SOPHIE.)

ROSE *(Very nervous).*   Oh. Good morning, Sophie.

SOPHIE.   We have seen each other earlier this morning, Mrs. Griggs.

ROSE.   Oh. It's like a nightmare to me, as if a year had gone by. I've asked for my breakfast tray twice and nobody pays any attention. And the doctor says that's the way it *must* be.

SOPHIE *(Exiting).*   I will get it for you.

ROSE *(Back at the window, speaks to* SOPHIE *who has left the room).*   Not you, Sophie. You have your own troubles, God knows. I don't know how any of us can eat anything today. (GRIGGS, *in riding pants and old shirt, comes in through the windows. Because she is upstage of the windows, he does not see her until she speaks)* I've been looking everywhere for you, Ben.

GRIGGS *(Turns).*   Rose. You knew where I was.

ROSE.   That was all we needed here today: a telephone call to the stables. Oh, Ben, it was I who found them. But you don't know about it —

GRIGGS.   I've heard all about it.

ROSE.   Terrible, isn't it?

GRIGGS.   Not very.

ROSE.   He's been a disappointment to me. I've been lying on the bed thinking about it. Nick Denery, I mean.

GRIGGS.   I'm sorry.

ROSE.   You know, Ben, I've just about come to the conclusion that I'm often wrong about people, mostly men.

GRIGGS.   And what did you and Henry — ah — put together, Rose?

ROSE.   It was so hot in town. Henry's got that wonderful air conditioning, of course, but it's never like your own air. I think Sunday's the hottest day of the year, anyway. Athalia's braces cost twenty-five hundred dollars at that Greek dentist's and believe me they don't make anybody look prettier —

GRIGGS.   What point did you come to about my decision?

ROSE.   Decision? Your decision —

GRIGGS *(Tensely)*.   Please stop playing the fool. I'm afraid of you when you start playing that game.

ROSE.   *You* afraid of *me?*

GRIGGS.   Yes, me afraid of you. This very minute. Be kind, Rose, and tell me what has been decided for me.

ROSE *(Softly, very nervous)*.   It wasn't like that. Before I saw Henry I went to see Dr. Wills. You know he won't ever see patients on Sunday.

GRIGGS.   Not unless the fee is over a hundred.

Rose. I've always been sorry you didn't like Howard Wills. He's known as the best man in the South,
Ben. He gave up a beach picnic with that woman, you
know. Only that famous a man could buck having an
open mistress —

Griggs. I don't want to hear about Wills. Come
to the point. What did you and Henry —

Rose (*Grows sober, recognizing the tone*). I've
been uneasy. I've sometimes been in pain, all summer.
But I guess I knew because I guess I've known since
that army doctor in 1934 — I didn't want to talk about
it — (*Moves toward him, frightened*) I have bad heart
trouble, Ben.

Griggs (*After a second, as if he were sick*). Don't
play that trick, Rose. It's just too ugly.

Rose. I am not playing a trick. Wills wrote you a
letter about it.

*(She reaches in the pocket of her robe, hands
him a folded paper. He takes it from her, reads
it.)*

Griggs (*Violently*). How much did Henry pay
Wills for this?

Rose (*Gently, seriously*). It wasn't bought. Even
Henry couldn't buy it.

*(She turns, goes toward door, as if she were a
dignified woman.)*

Griggs (*Softly*). Tell me about it.

Rose. There isn't much to tell. I've known some
of it for years, and so have you. I just didn't know it
was this bad, or didn't want to. Wills says I must lead a

— well, a very different life. I'll have to go to the country somewhere and rest most of the day — not climb steps or go to parties or even see people much. I like people, I — Well, I just don't understand what I can do, except sit in the sun, and I hate sun — Oh, I don't know. He said worse than I am saying — I can't say it —

GRIGGS.   Yes. *(After a second)* I'm sorry.

ROSE.   I know you are. You've been my good friend. I'm frightened, Ben. I play the fool, but I'm not so big a fool that I don't know I haven't got anybody to help me. I pretend about the boys and what they're like but I know just as well as you do that they're not very kind men and won't want me and won't come to help me. *(With feeling)* And of course I know about Henry — I always have. I've got nobody and I'm not young and I'm scared. Awful scared.

GRIGGS.   You don't have to be.

ROSE *(Who is crying, very quietly)*.   Wills says that if I take good care I might be, probably will be, in fine shape at the end of the year. Please stay with me this year, just this year. I will swear a solemn oath — believe me I'm telling the truth now — I will give you a divorce at the end of the year without another word. I'll go and do it without any fuss, any talk. But please help me now. I'm so scared. Help me, please. One year's a lot to ask, I know, but —

(GRIGGS *comes to her, presses her arm.)*

GRIGGS.   Of course. Of course. Now don't let's speak of it again and we'll do what has to be done.

(She turns, goes out. He stands where he is.
A minute later, CROSSMAN *comes in, stares at*
GRIGGS *as if he knew something was wrong.*
Then he speaks casually.)

CROSSMAN. Seen Sophie?

GRIGGS *(As if it were an effort, idly).* In
the kitchen, I guess. Tough break for the kid, isn't
it?

CROSSMAN. Perhaps it isn't. I don't know.
(He watches as GRIGGS *takes out a cigarette and*
lights it. GRIGGS's *hands are shaking and as he*
puts out the match, he stares at them.)

GRIGGS *(Smiles).* My hands are shaking.

CROSSMAN. What's the matter?

GRIGGS. Worst disease of all. I'm all gone. I've
just looked and there's no Benjamin Griggs.

CROSSMAN *(After a second).* Oh, that. And you've
just found that out?

GRIGGS. Just today. Just now.

CROSSMAN. My God, you're young.

GRIGGS *(Laughs).* I guess I was. *(Slowly, carefully)*
So at any given moment you're only the sum of your
life up to then. There are no big moments you can
reach unless you've a pile of smaller moments to stand
on. That big hour of decision, the turning point in
your life, the someday you've counted on when you'd
suddenly wipe out your past mistakes, do the work
you'd never done, think the way you'd never thought,
have what you'd never had — it just doesn't come suddenly. You've trained yourself for it while you waited —

or you've let it all run past you and frittered yourself away. *(Shakes his head)* I've frittered myself away, Crossman.

CROSSMAN. Most people like us.

GRIGGS. That's no good to me. Most people like us haven't done anything to themselves; they've let it be done to them. I had no right to let it be done to me, but I let it be done. What consolation can I find in not having made myself any more useless than an Ellis, a Denery, a Tuckerman, a —

CROSSMAN. Say it. I won't mind. Or a Crossman.

GRIGGS. The difference is you've meant to fritter yourself away.

CROSSMAN. And does that make it better?

GRIGGS. Better? Worse? All I know is it makes it different. Rose is a sick woman. But you know I'm not talking only about Rose and me, don't you?

CROSSMAN. I know.

GRIGGS *(Very slowly).* I am not any too sure I didn't partly welcome the medical opinion that made it easier for me to give up. *(Then in a low voice as if to himself)* And I don't like Rose. And I'll live to like her less.

(He starts toward door. CONSTANCE *appears in the hall carrying a tray. She is followed by* SOPHIE *who is carrying a carpet sweeper and a basket filled with cleaning rags, etc.* CONSTANCE *comes to the door. She speaks wearily.)*

CONSTANCE *(To* GRIGGS*).* Sorry about Rose's breakfast. I forgot it. Sophie is going to help Rose to get packed. I don't mean to sound inhospitable but since you were going tomorrow, anyway — *(Gently)* I'm just tired and it would be easier for us. Please forgive me but you're an old friend and you will understand.

GRIGGS *(Smiles, pats her arm).* I'll take the tray. *(He takes it from her, goes up the steps.* CONSTANCE *comes in the room, sighs, sits down.)*

CROSSMAN. Sophie. (SOPHIE *comes to him)* I was asked to give you this.

(He hands her an envelope.)

SOPHIE. Thank you, Mr. Ned.

CONSTANCE *(Idly, without much interest).* Secrets?

CROSSMAN. That's right. Secrets. Old love letters or something.

*(SOPHIE *laughs, goes out.)*

CONSTANCE *(After a silence).* I hate this house to-day.

CROSSMAN. Well, they'll all be gone soon.

CONSTANCE. You won't go? Please.

CROSSMAN. I'll stay for a few days if you'd like me to.

CONSTANCE. Oh, yes. I need you to stay.

CROSSMAN *(Points out of window).* Don't worry about what the town thinks. Just act as if nothing had happened and they'll soon stop talking.

CONSTANCE. Oh, I'm not worrying about that. *(Pauses)* I feel so lost, Ned. As if I distrusted myself, didn't have anything to stand on. I mean, right now, if you asked me, I just wouldn't know what I thought or believed, or ever had, or — *(Shyly)* Well, what *have* I built my life on? Do you know what I mean?

CROSSMAN. Sure. I know.

CONSTANCE *(As if she had trouble with the words).* It's — it's so painful. *(Then as if she wished to change the subject quickly)* Sophie will be going back to Europe. She just told me. She *wants* to go. Did you know that?

CROSSMAN. Is that so?

CONSTANCE. I was so sure I was doing the right thing, bringing her here. You see? That's part of what I mean by not knowing the things I thought I knew. Well. She wants me to come with her and live with them, but I told her I'd be no happier in a new life than she was. *(Pauses as if she were coming to something that frightens her)* Nick said you wouldn't be coming here next summer. Did you say anything like that, or was it one of Nick's lies? *(He does not answer her. She stares at him)* Why, Ned?

CROSSMAN. Hasn't anything to do with you, Con. Just think I'd be better off. You know, it's kind of foolish—two weeks a year—coming back here and living a life that isn't me anymore. *(Laughs)* It's too respectable for me, Con. I ain't up to it anymore.

CONSTANCE. Oh. It's what I look forward to every summer. What will I — *(Very quickly)* Where is Nick? I haven't seen him. I wish they'd leave —

CROSSMAN. They've gone.

CONSTANCE *(Stares at him).* Without a word to

me? Exactly the way he left years ago. I didn't ever tell you that, did I? We had a date for dinner. He didn't come. He just got on the boat. I didn't ever tell anybody before. *(Violently)* What a fool. All these years of making a shabby man into the kind of hero who would come back some day all happy and shining —

CROSSMAN. Oh, don't do that. He never asked you to make him what he wasn't. Or to wait twenty years to find him out.

CONSTANCE. No, he didn't. That's true. *(She rises, goes to the portrait and stands staring at it)* Do I look like this?

CROSSMAN. You look nice.

CONSTANCE. Come and look at it.

CROSSMAN. No. I don't want to.

CONSTANCE. Much older than I thought or — And I don't look very bright. *(Puts the picture away from her)* Well, I haven't been very bright. I want to say something to you. I can't wait any longer. Would you forgive me?

CROSSMAN. Forgive you? For what?

CONSTANCE. For wasting all these years. For not knowing what I felt about you, or not wanting to. Ned, would you have me now?

CROSSMAN *(After a second)*. What did you say?

CONSTANCE. Would you marry me? *(There is a pause. Then* SOPHIE *comes from the direction of the dining room carrying a carpet sweeper and a cleaning basket. As she goes up the steps she is singing a cheerful French song.* CONSTANCE *smiles)* She's happy. That's good. I think she'll come out all right, always.

CROSSMAN *(Stares at Constance, then slowly, carefully).* I live in a room and I go to work and I play a game called getting through the day while you wait for night. The night's for me — just me — and I can do anything with it I want. There used to be a lot of things to do with it, good things, but now there's a bar and another bar and the same people in each bar. When I've had enough I go back to my room — or somebody else's room — and that never means much one way or the other. A few years ago I'd have weeks of reading — night after night — just me. But I don't do that much anymore. Just read, all night long. You can feel good that way.

CONSTANCE.   I never did that. I'm not a reader.

CROSSMAN *(As if he hadn't heard her).*   And a few years ago I'd go on the wagon twice a year. Now I don't do that anymore. And I don't care. *(Smiles)* And all these years I told myself that if you'd loved me everything would have been different. I'd have had a good life, been worth something to myself. I wanted to tell myself that. I wanted to believe it. Griggs was right. I not only wasted myself, but I wanted it that way. All my life, I guess, I wanted it that way.

CONSTANCE.   And you're not in love with me, Ned?

CROSSMAN.   No, Con. Not now.

CONSTANCE *(Gets up, goes to him).*   Let's have a

nice dinner together, just you and me, and go to the movies. Could we do that?

CROSSMAN.   I've kept myself busy looking into other people's hearts so I wouldn't have to look into my own. *(Softly)* If I made you think I was still in love, I'm sorry. Sorry I fooled you and sorry I fooled myself. And I've never liked liars — least of all those who lie to themselves.

CONSTANCE.   Never mind. Most of us lie to ourselves, darling, most of us.

CURTAIN